The Write Stuff

Ray and Bevy Jaegers

Published by

krause
publications

700 E. State Street • Iola, WI 54990-0001
Telephone: 715/445-2214

Please, call or write us for our free catalog of antiques and collectibles
publications. To place an order or receive our free catalog, call 800-258-0929.
For editorial comment and further information,
use our regular business telephone at (715) 445-2214

Library of Congress Catalog Number: 99-68136
ISBN: 0-930625-86-2

Printed in the United States of America

TABLE OF CONTENTS

DEDICATION

To all those who have helped, guided, and assisted us in the pursuit of our collections – our thanks.

To Lance Daniel, who began the whole thing, to Nancy Olsen, Leonard Lipic, Ed Froelich, Glen Bowen, our friends at Pen World, Sandy Patrick, Angel Brennan, Alan Miller, our long-suffering editor, and most of all, to those who have been so willing to share – our very best.

SPECIAL THANKS

We especially want to thank all who contributed time, effort, photos, encouragement and support, and material for the book. Special thanks to Masa Sunami of Japan, Mary Rose Cahn, John D. Jaegers, D.J. Kennedy, Nancy Olson of Pen World, Vince McGraw, and all those who graciously shared their expertise and snapshots of their own collections.

Our deepest thanks to Angel Brennan, and Sandy and Mike Patrick whose skills were beyond price.

INTRODUCTION

Nine-tenths of human history, some say, has been written in flint. The rest has been written in ink. The stone tools of Cro Magnon and Neanderthal are studied and their cave paintings read by knowledgeable eyes. Is it so strange that we study and collect the implements with which all writing was done?

A sketch of a man carrying a weapon near a mammoth may have conveyed the same meaning a sign on a modern highway might, such as "deer crossing" or some other warning. We know the message was important enough for someone to crawl into a cave with a crude torch and paint it on a rocky surface with ochre and charcoal. Unfortunately, the specific meanings of these pictographs have been lost.

A particular set of cave paintings near Lascaux, France was once thought only to be an artistic expression of its maker. Later, the paintings were recognized as possibly the first expression of sequential thought. Early primitive cultures were seeking to record the animals amongst which they lived and hunted. They were also attempting to pass on information through these pictures. In the Lascaux series, a man accompanies a herd of animals. In many of the paintings the man is disguised as one of the herd. A shaman may have been giving instruction in methods of infiltration and sneak attack.

Over time, these crude attempts at depicting concepts became the raw beginnings of writing. A writing system, referred to as a script or orthography, consists of a set of visible marks, forms, pictographs, or characters, related to some structure in the language. Most commonly they are related to a particular sound.

A more enduring record reinforced thoughts and ideas previously passed on only through speech. As this process evolved, writing had to move from stone or plaster walls to portable, disposable surfaces such as clay tablets, rolls of leather, and waxen blocks. Quite recently, discoveries of early written records, such as the Dead Sea Scrolls, have been found in many places in the Middle East. Amazingly, they are as readable now as when first written.

Many materials were used as writing instruments, including bruised reeds, pointed sticks, brushes, and copper stylus-like instruments. Paints and inks were developed from natural juices, dyes, soot, and later from oak galls in Europe. Wooden and metal stylus instruments were used to scratch letters into wax or clay tablets. Clay tablets had to be baked in order to create a more permanent document. Wax was somewhat problematic as it could be smoothed over — a bad thing if you were a king and had a deceitful secretary or one who didn't agree with your latest decree. Other writing surfaces included parchment, rice paper, papyrus, and even cloth. Cloth required treatment with either wax or certain plant juices, which would prevent the ink from spreading.

Pictographic forms of writing such as Egyptian hieroglyphics are among the oldest in human history. Dating as far back as 3000 B.C., hieroglyphics first conveyed ideas, and later actual words. A glyph of a duck might have stood for a river, wetlands hunting, or the duck may have been eaten at the Queen's banquet. Hieratic writing was developed as a shorthand form of hieroglyphics, evolving from the more abstract glyph symbols into actual sounds and words. Modern shorthand systems, such as Gregg, trace their roots back to hieratic writing.

Alphabets originated in the Middle East around 2000 B.C. Unlike hieroglyphics, each letter or character in an alphabet was intended to represent a sound in the spoken language. As writing systems developed and changed, many of the meanings of the ancient world were lost or became indecipherable.

Not everyone could write or read in earlier centuries. Those who could were given the title of "scribe." We still use several forms of this ancient word: script, prescription, subscription, and manuscript to name a few. An early Egyptian tale of about 3000 B.C. lauds the ability to communicate through reading and writing.

A scribe, taking his son to school, compares the superiority of his profession with other tradesmen they pass:

"Look son, a blacksmith. He'll never attend at court. All day long he sweats and kneels at his hot furnace. Over there is a stonemason. All day he chips and wrestles with hard stone. He must sleep doubled up because of his aching back and arms. Look at Atef across the way, he is a barber and shaves people from dawn to dusk, wearing out arms and fingers just to fill his stomach. See that farmer leading his beasts? He slaves all day in mud or filth, never resting until the sun goes down. Therefore, son, give all your attention to the use of the writing reed and your letters, for truly, nothing compares with it for providing a comfortable life. If you succeed at school, it is a gain for eternity."

Eternity it was, for these first forms of written communication are still readable today, offering insight into the actions and thoughts of daily life in ages past.

Egypt, a land shrouded in mystery and magic, existed for thousands of years by the Nile. The forces of Imperial Rome absorbed this ancient empire just before the modern Christian era. Not many writing tools of ancient Egypt have survived, but a few papyrus scrolls find their way to Sotheby's and other fine auction houses. Such artifacts are generally out of the realm of most collectors, however. Most writing tools that have survived date from the 17th century and later. They are perhaps of greater beauty than the ancient pieces, which is where we come in.

Our first inkwell purchase was a lovely example in gilt and mother of pearl, but it was to be twenty-one years before my husband and I bought another, and that was purely an accident of proximity. Our collecting interests switched from dolls we could not afford, to antique and vintage fountain pens we could. We found that in addition to the pens available in malls and shops, a few other writing accoutrements often accompanied them.

At first we ignored these, blind to their charm. Eventually, as we found the carved ani-mals and other designs seductive, we began hesitantly to buy these accessories. We found the figural inkwells to be of intense interest, in their brass, bronze, and copper splendor. Gradually, these items began to impress themselves on our collector's "itch" and we added a few other items to the pile near the cash register or the auction payee desk.

In a short time, we owned an extensive collection of often unique and always fascinating items, about which we knew nothing. In those days there was practically no interest in pen-stands, desk items, old business machines, and dried-up commercial inkbottles. We were the blind being led by the blind. The dealers and auctioneers from whom we purchased these items knew little more than we did. As the collecting fever took firmer hold, we began to categorize our purchases and look for sources of information. We found little, but cherished what we could find.

In time, we decided what we would collect, and on which items we would concentrate. Already knowledgeable about a variety of fountain pens, we learned to clean and restore some of them. Early successes with these pens gave us the courage to buy other items which were not in mint condition, but which might yield to cleaning and a little T-L-C. We recommend that only an expert under take major restoration or repair. However, we have learned some simple techniques and practices, and include a chapter of care and restoration tips in this volume.

Collecting antiques is a fascinating, all-consuming interest. There is no better way to learn what is available than to shop and shop widely. Hands-on-experience is recommended; only in this way will you become knowledgeable. Within this book, we hope to offer what we have learned, no matter how little. We believe sincerely that cooperation is the best "yellow brick road" to expanding knowledge.

We're glad you're coming along on the journey...

CHAPTER 1

THE HISTORY OF INK AND INK CONTAINERS

The history of ink is fascinatingly complex, as is the story of its containers.

Early humans discovered that mixing soot and animal oils produced a semi-liquid substance that could be smeared onto cave walls or animal skins to make primitive pictures. These first efforts at writing, such as in the caves at Lascaux, are thought to be attempts at gaining power over the animals rather than telling a story.

Later cave pictures seem to be more realistic representations of hunting and human life. Red clay, ground and added to the black soot, pro-duced an ink-like substance. This combination was used on most cave paintings. Containers for these inks have not been identified, but were probably made from a hollowed stone or primitive clay pot.

In the days of the Egyptians, the art of writing reached a higher perfection on walls and tomb fixtures. Tomb paintings provided the dead with scenes from his or her life, as well as scenes from the Book of the Dead. These scenes contained long and complex methods for having one's life reviewed by several gods and goddesses. In addition to the wall paintings, papyrus

On the right is an example of a very early fired yellow clay well. Made since ancient times, clay wells were used by scribes in Egypt.

sheets were placed in tombs containing instructions for safe passage into the afterlife. Papyrus scrolls, written in hieratic script, were also used for commercial, religious, and royal communications.

The art of the scribe was born in ancient Egypt. Aristocratic families often employed their own scribes but Egyptian towns of any size had a scribe available to the public. Scribes used small ink palettes that were produced in rectangular pieces of stone with round hollows for each color of ink. There were usually three such hollows, one for red and two for the more essential black. Many of these portable ink-containers are still found. They were used with a dried form of ink that had to be mixed in the hollow of the stone with a bit of water, then brushed onto the surface with a reed or primitive brush

As writing progressed from the stylized hieroglyphic to the faster hieratic, it became necessary to keep a larger amount of ink ready. Clay and stone containers were used with wax stoppers to store the ink.

With the development of glass, the Egyptians began producing wells of this material in the same style as those formerly made of clay. Glass wells were only available to the nobility and upper classes, while lowly scribes still used clay or stone ink containers. Ink composition differed at this time, although the lampblack made from soot was still an important component.

Inkwells of these days were still strictly utilitarian bottles and containers with little ornamentation. Stoppers of beeswax or a piece of rag stuffed into the opening kept the ink from spilling or evaporating. As writing spread around the world, ink containers began to be made from animal horns. These containers were still used in pioneer and colonial days in the United States, especially because of their portability. Stretched skin was used over these horn containers to keep the ink from dripping out or evaporating from disuse. Oak gall ink, which became widely used when the trade route opened from England to China, is one of the main causes of disintegration of writing on documents of this era. The

highly acidic ink actually ate through the paper, making some older documents look like as though they were written on lace.

Legal documents have been executed in ink since ancient times. Continuous measures were taken to ensure the permanency of writing fluids on these documents. Pencils had to be relegated to the ranks of the unlettered and were prohibited from use on legal documents because signatures, amounts, and superscriptions in pencil were easily erasable. Ink, on the other hand, was erasable only by scraping the surface of the thick paper or parchment. The invention of Arabic ink, indelible ink, and other forms of difficult-to-erase ink awaited the 18th century. Even these inks, including India ink, are not completely indelible.

The Middle Ages and Renaissance saw the first ornamental inkwells, crafted in gold, electrum, silver, and other precious metals. Today, few of these inkwells and stands exist outside museum collections. Many are retained in the Vatican.

The Baroque period in Western Europe was characterized by an excessively ornamental style, while the Middle East retained the Moorish tray styles for which they were famed. With the landing of the Pilgrims at Plymouth Rock, these highly decorative inkstands became undesirable in the New World. The average household inkwell was more likely to be a stoneware bottle, while the gentry prized the sedate, stylized standish of silver.

A conflict of opinion exists concerning some early inkstands. Some of these have an extra container, a few having shaker holes in their lids. The conflict arises in not what they contained—sand or pounce—but for which purpose this was used. One school believes that the sand was shaken onto the parchment or paper to help dry the ink which otherwise would have smeared badly, as did some of Queen Elizabeth's desperate notes from the tower to her sister Mary. The second group holds that the sand or pounce was used as a sort of sandpaper to roughen the surface of the writing paper or parchment, so that it would accept the ink cleanly. I prefer the Hollywood scenario where the luckless king hastily scrawls a note as rebels pound down his door, and with a careless arm sweeps a layer of sand across the paper just before his trusted valet rolls it and tucks it into his sleeve. With the invention of blotting paper, an accidental byproduct of pulp milling in the 1800s, pounce became unnecessary.

A special tool was used to scratch out errors from the surface of the parchment after the ink had dried. The tool was usually a sharp piece of glass, metal, or stone that had an acutely angled edge which would scrape but not cut the paper. In the 1600s most lettered individuals owned a penknife. This tool had the dual purpose of cutting a quill from a feather properly, and also scraping errors off the paper surface. Some purists believe that such a tool has to accompany a writing set of the Middle Ages to late Colonial period in order to be authentic.

About the time of the Civil War, a portable inkwell was developed with a tiny spring inside. When the lid was unscrewed, a tiny glass vial popped up so that the pen could dip easily. When the top was again screwed down, the spring allowed the glass vial to sink into the depths of the small container. The spring also kept pressure against the top, preventing leakage. Usually plain and undecorated, these wells were carried by each literate soldier into battle so that he could write to his sweetheart if he survived. There are many varieties of such portable inkwells, but they are extremely difficult to find. In only a few is the spring still workable.

Queen Victoria's reign created a desire for excessive ornamentation once again. The gaudy or baroque inkwell, protected by hovering cherubs and cupids nestling amongst bowers of roses, came into fashion. Following the style of the day, painted porcelain was much desired. In most homes an inkwell or inkstand of this type was displayed somewhere in the drawing room. These were also the days of scented and highly colored inks, and lavender, pink, and orchid joined the color range. Crusty staid businessmen still preferred the stolid, unornamented double well. One side of the well contained the ordinary black ink; the other held the dreaded red. From this situation come the phrases "in the black" to denote success, and "in the red" to suggest a lack of funds.

At the beginning of the Art Nouveau era in the late nineteenth century, inkwells remained

Two examples of transitional late Victorian ink stands. On the left is a cherub backing a pen-rest in brass with ramped crystal well. The lid is made of Bakelite, one of the earliest plastic-type materials available. The well measures 8-1/2 inches by 4-1/2 inches. The well on the right is a brass double inkstand with Romanesque figures in relief, measuring 4 inches by 7 inches: $230.

9

The unusual relief work on this well is actually a family heraldic crest. The elements in the complicated design suggest origins in either Wales or Scotland. The animal on top of the helmet appears to be a hare. One of a kind pieces of this type were often cast in fine sand, then polished. The hinge-back conceals a glass insert. 3-1/3 inches high: $275.

fanciful and stylized. Beautiful maidens with flowing hair replaced the chubby cupids. Natural forms became predominant. Butterflies, oak leaves, iris blooms, and tree stumps were found on inkstands and wells of all materials. Some of the finest examples are in bronze, while equally attractive models are found in brass, copper, pewter, and even pot metal.

Souvenir inkwells became popular, and were made of a wide mix of materials. Seaside resorts specialized in inkwells carved from a single conch shell or a mother-of-pearl conch fashioned into the shape of a fish. Some of these were labeled with the name of the resort, but with use these cellophane labels have vanished or become unreadable. As tourism became an industry, architectural features were recreated in pot metals and papier-mâché, and were hawked from barrows in the bazaars of Europe.

Fine examples of woodcarving were produced in Germany for centuries. Some cottage industries still crafted these bears, gnomes, and

Two figural wells typical of the Victorian era. The pewter cherub well on the left has a hinge-backed top concealing the insert. $100. The Indian bust at right is made of a copper alloy and also has a hinged top: $140. Photo courtesy M. Sunami.

trees at the end of the nineteenth century. But as the twentieth century took hold, the level of craftsmanship dropped. Simple geometric shapes ornamented with chip carving took the place of the older owls and bears.

With the advent of the Art Deco style in the 1920s, the fountain pen began to eclipse the ink-well as an item of necessity. The few wells produced were likely to be strictly curvilinear in form. They were designed not for milady's secretary desk, but for the boss's desk and the clerk's writing stand. A few wells were produced in the basic turquoise and black, orange and black, and gold and black of the Art Deco style. Craftsmanship had declined drastically, and few examples survive from this era.

Inkwells reached their last stand in the years 1925 through 1935. Some comically ugly styles were produced either as tourist souvenirs or for the odd curmudgeon who insisted on using a dip pen and ink. Several of the larger pen companies ventured into the field with decorative bottles such as the Ma and Pa Carter pottery bottles.

Art Nouveau styling is evident in this piece marked in medium relief SBMA 1909 (St. Louis Business Association.) Made of dull pewter, it was produced during a period when pewter was regaining popularity. The floral lid pushes to one side to reveal a clear glass insert held in a collar: $150.

A true primitive, this carved wood inkstand could be of either European or early New England manufacture. The detailed nut is hinged to reveal a tiny insert, which was made of either glass or metal, or the wood was treated to retard the absorption of fluid ink. This very early 18th century model has its insert. With insert: $95, without: $75.

Huge and imposing, this double-inkstand handcrafted of wood measures 15-1/2 inches in length, 9-1/2 inches deep, and 7 inches high. It will dwarf anything, but a large library table or roll-top desk. Large double crystal wells with petal adorned wooden tops flank a carved wood scroll. The lettering on the scroll in front of the owl is German, "Frau Lehn wien 2" (wien vieuve), suggesting Austrian manufacture: A piece of this size and workmanship is valued at $800 and up.

Unusual coloring marks these Ma & Pa Carter inks which were produced for only two years. The heads on the figural bottles acted as lids for their inkwell bodies. The brilliant orange is reminiscent of prewar Japanese manufacture, as are the slippers on the Pa figure's foot. $150 each in excellent condition.

A more modern ink available in Japan, a large reservoir hinge-lidded ink in wonderful condition: $85-$100. Photo courtesy of Ray & Miriam Call.

The Parker Pen Company produced an all-in-one inkwell, pen-stand, and calendar-holder reminiscent of the prewar era in which it was made. Sold with a green-shaded lamp, it could transform a cubbyhole into an office with its gleaming contours.

The shift to the use of the convenient, all-in-one fountain pen hastened the demise of the ink well. No longer was the decorative and functional well needed at the desk. Ink was still a necessity, but it could now be directly put into the fountain pen, where it might last for the writing of many pages before needing replenishing.

Today's artists use India ink as two of these common bottles contain. Many pour their ink into a Skrip bottle for more convenience.

13

CHAPTER 2

FROM STONE TO SHELL: INKWELL MATERIALS

Inkwells have existed as long as written history. From simple rounded depressions in stone, where powdered inks could be ground and mixed with liquid, to the elaborate precious metal inkwells and inkstands of the Victorian era, inkwells have been essential throughout history. Inkwells have been made from a variety of materials. The earliest wells were strictly utilitarian and made from stone and clay. As new materials were discovered and new techniques developed for working them, the variety of inkwells increased. Nearly any material capable of holding ink has been used to produce wells at some time or other.

STONE

Stone was a logical choice of material for early inkwells. Readily available in most areas of the globe, suitable types provided a non-porous container for the ink. The earliest containers utilized a naturally occurring hollow in the stone to hold the ink. Later, wells were made by chipping and carving the stone.

Probably because of availability, there are many American inkstands and desk stands made of soapstone, which has a somewhat greasy feel. Onyx, travertine marble, and other stone materials were also used to make inkwells. They are correspondingly heavy, some so much so that

This beautiful inkstand, made of colorful red, white, and black onyx, was made in the late 18th century. The double inkwells conceal pottery inserts beneath hinge-backs. 16 inches by 9 inches and massive: $160.

An unusual inkwell carved of red soapstone carries an advertisement for a stone quarry: $50.

they would be beyond the ability of a child or some women to pick up easily.

Just as their material is denser than other desk items, the styling of stone inkwells is more severe. Generally squared off and massive in effect, few of these impressive pieces are marked.

POTTERY

Fired or baked earthen or clay containers for ink go back into the dawn of history. Pottery ink containers may range from a mere 150 years to more than a thousand years in age. Some civilizations, such as the ancient Egyptians and Greeks, produced pottery using sophisticated techniques thousands of years ago. These pieces may have been thrown on a wheel, fired in kilns, and glazed. Other societies produced more primitive pottery. These were often made of unglazed earthenware and crudely shaped. Without using sophisticated dating methods, it is often difficult to judge the age of pottery wells.

Another massively heavy soapstone inkstand. Double hinge backs on the wells conceal glass and metal inserts. The two pen-holders in the tray are souvenir pieces from Niagara Falls and Sedalia Missouri. Ink stand measures 13 inches by 12 inches: $225.

15

These wells are of the oldest type of fired wells. Made for thousands of years, on every continent where writing flourished, they are becoming increasingly hard to find in perfect condition.
Left: Primitive yellow clay well: $20-$50.
Center: Pouring bottle from England, 7 inches tall: $50.
Right: Oldest of the three wells pictured, this red clay example has a 1 inch diameter opening: $30.

Ink, by its very nature, had to be kept liquid while in use. It was difficult to keep for any length of time in an unglazed container, although a stone container might keep it liquid for a day or so. Pressed into a flat cake or small square, it might be found on a makeshift palette or in an Egyptian scribe's writing case.

Production of pottery, faience, majolica, and other glazed forms of ink containers proliferated tremendously in the seventeenth and eighteenth centuries. At this time, methods of pottery production improved, making it easier to produce more wells. At the same time, writing ability spread beyond the privileged classes increasing the demand for inkwells. The use of ink containers parallels the ability of the common man to first read and then to write. With this more universalized communication, ink containers became items for trade with other societies, within local areas, and even across oceans.

At this point, decoration became more desirable. The humble and primitive round or geometric shapes metamorphosed into containers of increasing color, style, and variety. Home ink containers were much more likely to be colorful, imaginative, and breakable, while those found in business establishments tended to be more staid. Examples of pottery wells provide a look not only at the styles of the period during which they were produced, but also provide a very personal glimpse into the actual home in which they were used.

Ships full of pottery followed trade routes to the United States and beyond, spreading widely through the entire continent. Naturally, the greatest variety of inkwells will be discovered in the Eastern states as they were settled earliest. However, the number of wells diminishes only slightly as the great Mississippi divides the land. Only in the vast grasslands of the Western states

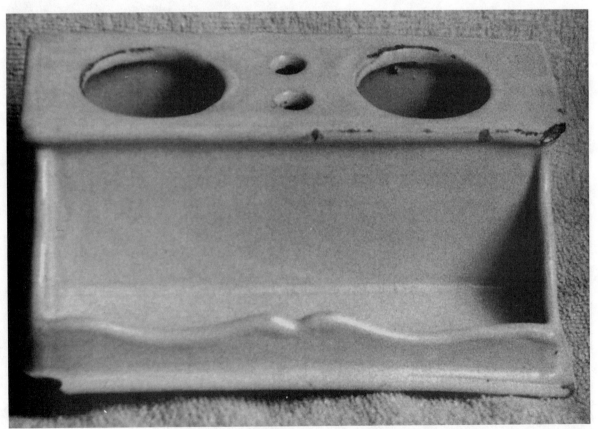

Simple majolica inkstand. The two larger holes held containers for ink, sand, or pounce. The smaller openings are for quills, and the front tray held tools. Stand measures 8 inches by 3 inches: $110.

are inkwells less common. Even there a rare find may be made; perhaps the fruit of some emigrants overloaded Conestoga wagon..

American potters were quick to add saleable inkwells and bottles to their line of local clay products. The famous companies of Bennington, Vermont, such as U.S. Pottery and the American Pottery Manufacturing Company, may have actually tipped on their mark in addition to producing distinctive colors and glazes.

Smaller local potteries began producing graniteware, flintware, redware, yellowware, and a variety of other styles, glazed and unglazed, as the 1800s began. Some are marked, some are not, and some marks are untraceable. Prices for these styles, which are either more decorative or even extremely whimsical in form, range from less than $50 to more than $250.

Perhaps it is the very youth of the United States that makes many inkwells and unmarked containers more difficult to place and date. Styles of manufacture, decoration, and materials, which would be familiar to an Italian or a French collector, are often extremely hard for an American dealer or buyer to identify and price. This results in some rare and very valuable "finds" at malls and garage sales for literally pennies. While a simple marked specimen may be unrealistically high in price on a dealer's shelf, those unmarked specimens may be collected with a much smaller budget.

Chips are extremely common on pottery containers, especially on glazed pieces. Since pottery has a tendency to chip more than does porcelain, the quality along with the price is often damaged considerably. A small "chigger bite" will not necessarily reduce the price by half. However, if the styling is ordinary and the painting simple, this will be the case. If, how-

Marked "Medullae Patent 1859." This gravity fed well is of French manufacture with brass accommodations. Ink is forced into the side chamber by a heavy weight suspended in a larger chamber. A thin brass plate is attached as lid of dip chamber. Stoneware: $400 .

Camark pottery well of lustrous black and gold. Of their most desirable curved, almost combed-ribbed styling, and frosted in gold, this beehive inkwell has a cork-rimmed stopper cap. Not very efficient in terms of ink capacity, the well measures five inches tall and is delightfully heavy. Red clay base. Very high glaze, rarely seen: $295.

ever, the style is exceptional and the artistic elements are fine, a small defect in the paint or a tiny chip will not ruin the value of a fine piece. Often a display of such wells or stands can be arranged on a shelf and the small defect placed to the rear, thus making it less obvious to the eye.

Cracks are also only too common on pottery wells. Many wells and bottles were discarded outdoors or tossed into unheated sheds. Exposed to extremes of temperature, these containers suffered cracking and discoloration. Some cracks may not lower the value of a well-made example too much, but chips will generally cut the price

Group of larger master ink bottles.
Far Left: Early stoneware bottle with pour spout, fired and blackened 7 inches: $50.
Left: Tan 6 inches screw top: $20-30.
Right: Red-ware bottle corked pulled lip 9 inches: $30.
Far Right: "Levinson blue black" white stoneware with remnants of paper label. $35-$50.

by one quarter to one half. If the well is meant only to be an example of a type, these considerations may be less harmful to the price. Some of the same rules that cover early crocks also pertain to clay and pottery wells, which may be collected for the style and maker rather than condition.

Pottery wells are slower than those made of metal to be reproduced, except for the pricey semi-Staffordshire dog or semi-Wedgwood styling. These fakes are seen in increasing numbers, with pseudo-cracks and dust rubbed in to give the appearance of age. Inkstands or standishes are more likely to be faked than single inkwells. Generally the more decorative types suffer more from the reproduction fakers. To date, we have seen perhaps a hundred thousand examples of famed "mammy" or black memorabilia in cookie jars and salt and pepper shakers, but only a small number of reproduced inkwells.

The bottom of the well will betray its age, for the grinding of placement on a surface will

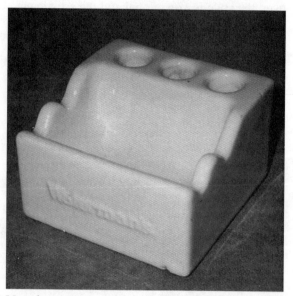

Very heavy stoneware piece. Possibly a Waterman Pen display, it is similar to a type commonly produced in many areas of New England from about 1810–1840: $175. Photo courtesy M. Sunami.

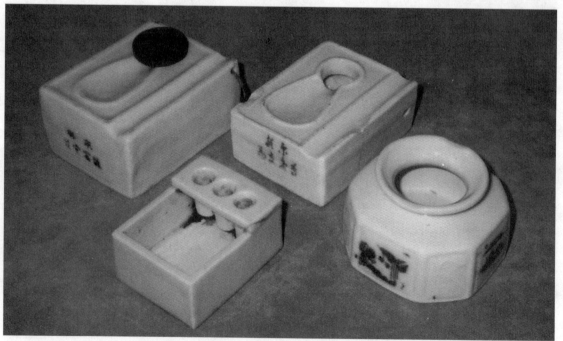

A group of Japanese-made pottery and china inkwells in the traditional blue and white. Valuation $25-$35 each in perfect condition. Photo courtesy M. Sunami.

20

roughen the circumference of the well's base and reveal wear. Markings can be trusted for the most part, even though most wells of clays had few or no marks at all.

Pottery wells are fascinating in their size and variety, as well as the range of color they provide. Even those of the plainest manufacture reveal surprising differences in materials and glazes. It is of value to collect these plainer wells while they are still inexpensive. Like any collectible, as demand increases for these wells so does their price. While the fancier wells are always more popular, the historian in us will inevitably be drawn to pick up the plainer Cinderella-type inkwells as they are a distinctive part of our past.

PORCELAIN

Many collectors are confused as to the difference between pottery and porcelain. Pottery is usually made of coarser, softer clay. When chipped, pottery has a rubbly texture. Porcelain, made from finer white clay, is translucent and much harder than pottery. Porcelain leaves a harder, sharper chip, due to the glassy overglaze.

The greatest number of porcelain works was imported to America from the Colonial era through the 1920s. Imports from the great makers of Austria, Bohemia, Italy, France, and England make up the largest number of surviving desk accessories, with the inkstand leading the pack. Imprints range from Limoges to Alcock, from Capo di Monte to Sareguemines. Royal Doulton, Worcester, and the wide variety of Continental styles almost always carry marks, which may be identified with the assistance of major mark-identification volumes.

Unfortunately, not all makers of porcelain wells or stands were so kind as to mark their product. At times, the styling itself acts as the maker's mark. At other times, the use of certain

A lovely example of a Staffordshire-type well, in cream-ware with gold highlighting. 5 inches by 2-7/8 inches with removable powder sander and ink insert: $295.

From Italy, this typical classic inkstand is marked with the N and Crest of Capo Di Monte. Polychrome and gold enamel work embellishes the elegant piece. 8 inches by 3-1/2 inches with double wells, non-hinged lids and double quill holes. Heavy relief decoration. If perfect: $1500.

This unusual curvilinear inkstand features an odd combination of shape from shell to scrolling in gold on white. The shell form was to hold quills steady in the tray. 1870s double porcelain inserts: $315.

"Old Paris" type porcelain inkstand with pierced pounce container lid and inkwell cover lid. This type was finished with fired-gold accents, and either hand-painted or embellished with transfer decorations. The rose transfer patterns on this stand are charming: $375.

motifs or colors, or the use of hard-paste porcelain may identify the maker more easily than an underglaze trademark. Buyers must be extremely careful of overglaze markings that are painted above the glassy fired surface. Some Japanese companies painted spurious trade-

Late 1940s China desk pieces were imported from Japan. These small 1-3/4 inch cube inkwells have been attributed to pre-war Joan, Lefton, and other makers. The inkwell is not uncommon, but the stamp box is rare. Hand painted. Two piece set: $50.

marks on their wares designed for export. An indication of these imposters is the quality of the glaze; it may be stippled with tiny flaws or embedded grit. Many Japanese companies produced porcelain pieces of great artistry and skill. These companies added their own trademarks, most notably the apple blossom, and the wreathed "M" of Morimura Brothers, later Noritake.

WOOD

Wood was among the first materials used to hold ink. Being absorbent, wood did not make the best of holders for liquid ink. However, when a liner was added to keep the ink from being absorbed, it was a workable material. Wood is widely available in almost all areas of the planet. Along with animal bone and ivory, wood formed the most common materials from which to make necessities before the wide use of metals. Wood was used to make inkwells until the 1920s when the Age of Plastics began.

Wooden inkwells and other desk tools are not as common today as are those made of other materials, because it is absorbent and tends to stain unless inserts of glass or metal were used.

These three inkwells range in age from 40 to 140 years of age. Designed for travel, their caps fit tightly to prevent leaks.
Left: Small black lacquered wood: $45.
Middle: Early Skrip traveler: $35.
Right: Thin carved wood of type commonly carried by soldiers in the Civil War and travelers on stagecoach or early steam trains. The glass insert sits upon a coiled wire spring which releases when top is unscrewed: $95 each and up. Much more if name exists on bottom.

The art of woodcarving is also not a common skill today. Most late period wood inkwells are strictly utilitarian. Some of these were produced during the Arts and Crafts period early in the twentieth century, and reflect the simplicity emphasized by that movement.

Not surprisingly, areas where wood is the most abundant produced many intricately carved wells and inkstands. The Black Forest area of Germany and Switzerland, as well as the Holy Land, produced many wooden inkwells at one time. American Colonists, finding forest materials common on the new shores, also produced a few.

Most of the more decorative of these wells were made either for home use by a carver or later as a cottage industry when European tour-

ism reached its height in the Victorian era. Such wells were often carved in high relief, and a large number featured animals and objects familiar to the woodcarver. A carved tree stump

Excellent example of woodcarving, depicting the popular bear. This bear has glass bead eyes and is actually the handle for a blotter: $70.

A more primitive example of carving is seen in this wooden rose well. The center petals hinge-back to reveal a very small insert. One of a kind folk art wells of this type often bring amazing prices at auction. 3-1/2 inches by 4-1/2 inches: $75-$300.

Chip-carved of European wood, this 1880s box is signed by the artist and usually found marked with the name of a German or Swiss tourist area. Nicely lacquered in clear varnish, the contrast of wood is harmonious. Hinge-back conceals a white porcelain insert: $150-$175.

Unusual in any collection, this rare inkwell hails from the Middle East. Its finely detailed floral decoration and knife stippling would make it attractive to any tourist! Hinge-backed lid opens to reveal a sunken glass insert, 3 inches in diameter, it is a gem of the carved art: $75-$90.

is often depicted, as are leaves and other forest motifs. When a cover was needed for the inkwell, a carved acorn might conceal the top of the well.

The interesting thing about such wooden inkwells is that for the most part these are unique in design and quality. Except for a short period in the late 1800s, when tourist items were being produced, they were rarely found in great numbers, and few are alike in style or size.

METALS

Silver

According to known records, the most prolific makers of metal inkwells ranged from silversmiths like the famed Paul Revere, to English firms both large and small. These precious metal creations are marked with imprinted hallmarks, easily looked up in reference books. Silver was only widely used as a medium for inkstands and wells around the time of the American Revolution. Silversmiths and goldsmiths had always produced splendid ornate pieces for royalty and the Church, but the common businessman tended not to want silver, which easily tarnished. Colonial times brought such prosperity that silver became popular amongst the gentry who had household help whose sole job might be polishing the family's silver.

Iron

Several of the iron-working companies on both sides of the Atlantic were involved in inkstand and inkwell production. The earliest iron wells were of wrought iron. Once the process was developed, most iron wells were of cast iron. Few companies marked their wells as to maker and place of origin, but some used tiny initials and indecipherable trademarks. In the case of the commonly found hotel inkwell of ironwork and glass, there is often a date, but no further identification. A thorough search of catalogs from the 1840s to 1880s does not add much

Hotel single inkwell with typical pen-stand and aluminum-like cap: $80.

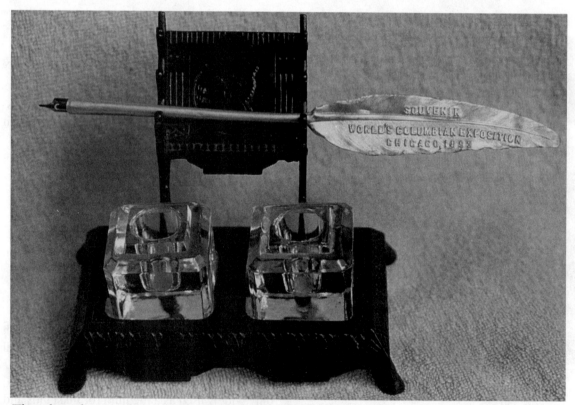

This inkstand is one of a group often known as "hotel wells" because they were produced in the 1860s for commercial enterprises including hotels and businesses. Most are painted black to cover the floral or swirled designs in low relief. This double set still contains its crystal wells and the triple penholder sports a commemorative silver dip pen from the Columbian Exposition of 1892-3. Stand: $85-$100, Pen: $75.

Another hotel type model, this one without pen-rest.
Press-cut glass wells with ironwork tops: $85-$105.

Most desired of this "snail" iron and glass 1800s
stand is the single snail, as double sets are more
numerous, Single: $125.

Iron and brass set with non-matching crystal wells. This may hve been intentional as the caps are
identical: $150-160 for this artistic set.

knowledge as to makers. One or more of the larger iron-working companies of Ohio or Pennsylvania probably produced the majority of iron wells. A few iron pieces are more distinctively European in styling, and were fabricated in England, France, or Germany for export.

Huge flanges at mold joint points, modern screw heads on the bottom, and garish paint slathered over the item by airbrush give away the recent origins of modern reproductions of these wells.

Brass

The most prolific maker of stands and wells of brass was the well-known firm of Bradley and Hubbard of Meriden, Connecticut. Their output ranged from staid, "business only" models to simple, yet tasteful designs adaptable to any home or salon decor. Their forte was in creating lamps for table and floor, as well as beautifully worked inkwells, inkstands, rocker blotters, letter knives, and other associated desk pieces. Their distinctive style is easily recognized, and

Artistically the English were supreme in Victorian brass-work of this type. The handled tray seems designed for royalty and perhaps it was. Double glass wells are concealed by hinge-back finish of baroque styling: $1100.

Heavy brass Art Nouveau styling with the flowing curvilinear styling of the period characterizes this piece. The metal-shelled inkwell is very unusual: $280.

A brass railing surrounds the hinge-back brass single well, on a marble base The racking is designed to hold a pen while it dries. 7 inches by 7 inches: $85.

Simple brass tray with crystal inkwell, cap, and stamp box: $70.

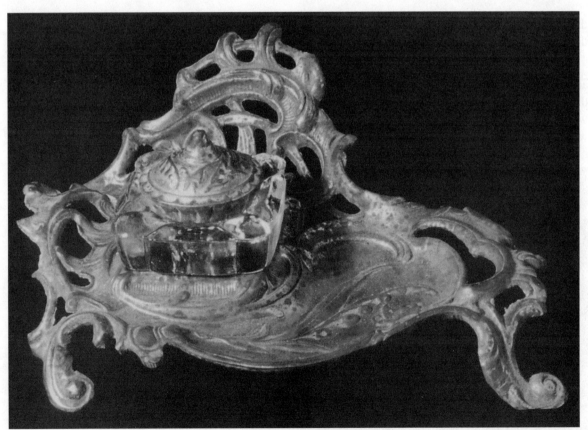

In a style popular from 1870-1890, this brass and glass example provides a pen-rest above its petal-footed tray. A brass lid completes the act: $150-175. Note: A similar type with sprays of lily of the valley on the tray is being reproduced and sold as original, BEWARE.

Double acorn finials crown the openwork brass of this exquisite inkstand. The quadruple-legged tray is most distinctive, as are the lovely cobalt blue ink cups concealed behind the heavy worked overlay. Probably of European make, it is truly unique: $3000.

they were careful to add their mark "B & H" or the Aladdin-Lamp trademark to their wares.

Many other makers in America and in Europe added to the number of brass wells. Brass has the odd quality of being the single other metal which, when polished properly, looks as if it were really made of gold. If not sealed with a coating, brass soon loses this golden luster. Modern collectors must always be careful not to use a cleaner, which will damage or remove this coating.

Bronze

Bronze was a metal of choice as it was considered more elegant than brass, did not rust like

A Bradley and Hubbard well of pinkish bronze. Art Deco utility and functionality are combined in a massive single well: $150-$200.

On ball feet, this bronze stand is deceptively simple in styling. It is a factory model measuring 6 inches by 6 inches: $65.

iron, and was often covered with a thin protective coat that would darken, but not flake off. Bradley and Hubbard produced many inkwells and other desk pieces in bronze. Other companies produced bronze wells of fine styling but unfortunately few of these wells were marked.

In addition, many foreign makers made bronze work that has survived and can add much

A light bronze single well on four tab feet. Pure Art Deco styling on base and sides is capped with a daisy sunburst on the hinged top, which conceals a white glass insert. Unusual blending into almost pure copper color at the edges is an eye-catcher. 6 inches by 4 inches: $190.

An enormous inkstand designed only for the desk of an executive (or a writer) provides crystal inkwells that hold a half-pint of ink. This light-bronze piece is almost breathtakingly exquisite in style. Made in 1890-1900, it has an aura of sheer elegance. No country of origin is determined, but the octagonal glass wells show an element of the Continental. Truly unique! 8 by 12 inches: $2500-$3000.

The architectural styling of Bradley & Hubbard is evident in this weighty piece. Its almost cenotaph-like lines are softened by the arched struts of the pen-rests on each side. In Meriden, Connecticut, this firm made bronze items from 1876 to the 1920s. This example is from the middle years. The heavy hinge-back opens to reveal a white glass insert: $420.

The design of this well shows once more the basic architectural styling of Bradley and Hubbard in its unusual geometric forms. Softening was often added to such stylized pieces such as the bronze-wire pen supports on both sides of this piece. It is elements like these that add so much to the Bradley & Hubbard charm: $375-$410.

A transitional piece at the end of the Art Nouveau and beginning of the Art Deco period, this pod-footed design owes much to both and hallmarks its age at 1920-25. If one looks very closely, a fleur de lis is concealed in the exuberant foliage. Probably from France, this 12 inch by 12 inch piece is valued at $400.

Bronze and crystal single wells of this sort are seldom complete. 4 inches by 3 inches: $140.

to a collection. In France, several makers specialized in Art Nouveau styled pieces, often embellished with animal or bird figures of exquisite modeling.

Late 18th Century gilt French lady's well with paper-thin mother of pearl insets in the tripod support. Small pressed glass 1 inch insert with a loosely fitted floral cap: $325.

Gilt

Some few wells, especially of English make, are made of cheap "pot metal" with a very thin layer of gold overlaid. Pot metal is an alloy of tin and other base metals. The gold overlay is negligible, and only added in the final stage of the process. These wells are seldom marked, and almost always of English or Continental manufacture. My first inkwell purchase was a gilt piece. Three lovely ovals of mother of pearl, perfectly matched in curve and arch, embellish this fine piece. Had it really been made of gold, its value might be in the thousands of dollars rather than hundreds. Much of this gilt work was also produced in the south of France and along the Mediterranean coast.

Vermeil

Combinations of gold overlaid on silver, or silver overlaid on gold began to be produced in Europe in the seventeenth century or earlier. Tiffany and Bradley and Hubbard continued this practice on a small scale for their more moneyed clientele. Our own collection does not concentrate upon this type of well, as we have tried to buy wells we like because of exceptional styling or some figural element. Few vermeil products were of the figural type.

Tin

Few wells were made of tin, due to the metal's fragility and tendency to rust. These same qualities meant that few tin wells survived. Tole is one of the most prevalent styles of tin wells. This style is characterized by colorful brushwork on a flat black background.

Some effigy styles made in the shape of a church, cathedral, or building are actually made of tin, lead or antimony, but only chemical testing will tell which.

Immediately prior to the World War II era, Japanese makers tried to enter the souvenir field with inkwells of their own. We do have one of these in our collection, which features cherry blossoms and musical notes as a part of its obviously tourist-designated style. These, however, were made far too late in the game for popularity. By the late 1930s, fountain pens had almost entirely eclipsed the inkwell. Very few examples of this type exist and they are extremely difficult to locate.

Tole-ware in inkwells is extremely unusual. This Greek-influenced urn holds a pair of small capacity wells and a lidded compartment for wax seal wafers. The rings, suspended from each end of the 7 inch width, are puzzling and may have been added to provide artistic balance. Gold stenciling on tin, probably made 1840-60: $250.

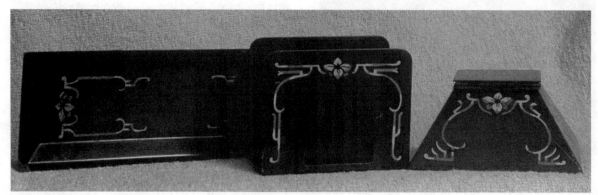

A rare toleware set with typical Victorian stenciling designs. Set $165. Individual pieces: inkwell $90, letter rack $30, and pen tray $30-$35.

The mysterious turquoise blue and black inkwell is on the right. Some speculate that this may have been an ashtray, not an inkwell: $40.

Aluminum

Aluminum, the most abundant metal in the Earth's crust, was not commercially produced until the late 1880s. This light, durable, and easily worked metal was especially popular during the Art Deco decade of the 1920s. Aluminum wells were often embellished with colorful sectors of red and black, blue and black, or other deco-inspired color combination in enamel.

We own one questionable item in this category, which is most probably an inkwell with a pushback cover, in turquoise and black deco quadrants. A small but nagging question exists, however, as to whether it may have been meant as an ashtray.

Until another example is found, perhaps as part of a smoking set, or a desk set, we will call it an inkwell.

Most unusual tin inkstand from Japan with impressed musical notes, Mt. Fuji in high relief, and what looks like a bouquet of cherry blossoms on the tray. On the hinge-back well, a moon rises over a mountain. A very unusual piece: $75.

Chrome

Another unusual category is found in the tiny group of wells produced in chromed steel. Brilliant and enduring, these styles are also often reminiscent of the Deco era. Several of them are of obvious Oriental or Eastern make, which can be puzzling, as the Deco influence did not often extend itself into the more heavily styled designs of Asian manufacture.

Chrome was also sometimes used as a styling decoration for wells made of other metals. Here again, the overall impression is that of the twenties or Deco era. Chrome pieces, when you find them, may also be enhanced by an overlay of brilliant color enamel.

GLASS INKWELLS

One of the largest categories of inkwells, if not inkstands, is the glass category. From earliest times to the years just before World War II, glass formed at least part of three out of every five inkwells produced.

Steuben glass well with bronze hinged lid with tip-lever. 3-1/2 inches tall, 4-1/2 inches diameter. Marked: $350.

Makers ranged from the great glass houses of Italy and France to the more colorful styles of Czechoslovakian make. In America, Steuben

Left: Blown clear glass well irregular lip: $15.
Center: Octagonal blown molded well in teal. 3 inches: $40.
Right: Bottle glass blown molded well, paneled sides for label, no lip: $30.

Three different basic roll-proof inks, blown molded with rolled lips.
Left: Aqua: $20.
Center: Deep Green with mold mark: $20.
Right: Light olive green: $15.

Three styles of blown funnel wells.
Left: Cobalt blown in mold. 1-7/8 inches: $40.
Center: Hand blown gray-green 1700s prototypical. 1-1/8 inches: $35.
Right: Clear glass. 1-13/16 inches: $15.

was known to have produced a number of lead crystal inkwells of great weight. Every other glassmaker produced at least one or two examples of inkwells. Many of these can be identified by the glassmaker's distinctive markings on the bottom of the piece.

Glass bottles and wells were generally formed by one of three methods: blown, blown-molded, or molded. Early bottles were hand-blown by skilled glass blowers. A clear unmistakable "ponty" or pontil mark on the base indicates that a bottle was made using the freehand method. Cheaper bottles might have the distinctive imprint of the straw heap upon which they were thrown to cool after being cut loose from the glassblower's rod. The interest in these early blown bottles is in the variety of shapes and colors of glass. Colors were determined by the amount of minerals contained in the molten glass from which they were blown. Prime desirability here is any color of blue, from the intensity of cobalt to the intriguing combinations of

blue and green which range from turquoise to teal blue and may be of intense hue or pastel tint. Red and pink are next on the list, closely followed by purple and lavender. Brown, amber, and opaline form the next group, while chalk white and clear hit the bottom unless they are of exceptional styling, or have pen-rests molded into the blower's design.

White and clear bottles are likely to be in the blown-molded category. These were produced by a glassblower blowing his hot metal while holding part of it within a mold of material ranging from sand to wood. A sand mold will not leave easily distinguishable mold marks, while molds of any other material will, if only upon the bottom of the bottle's sides. To remove these would have required fire finishing, an additional step adding time to the process. Most glassmaking houses therefore did not often add it.

Pouring molten glass directly into molds was the method used to form molded bottles and wells. A mold-mark will usually be visible at

Left: Early bottle glass well with two pen- rests. 3 inches by 2-3/4 inches: $30.
Right: Unusual opaque milk glass well with applied lip. $28.

Very unusual clear double well, apparently molded in sand. Label remnant "NK" on base: $35.

least on the neck of the bottle. Collectors prize blown three-mold bottles and wells. A careful study of any of the books on glass-blown items will give the collector a familiarity with features that will distinguish the differences between the above categories, as well as those which differentiate the mouth or lip of these glass products.

Later products were almost entirely made of molded or poured glass as they could be made quickly and inexpensively. A tendency to make wells of squared-off bottom and lid overtook the field, and it is difficult to tell one maker's product from another's. In the latter half of the nineteenth century, many glass makers began producing pattern glass tableware. Many makers also produced inkwells in pattern glass designs. Without a glass mark, or distinctive glass patterning, they could be the products of any of a hundred glass houses.

Group of four clear glass wells.
Far left: 1 inch paneled with 'stretched' lip: $10-$15.
Left: Ring-shouldered Waterman's: $7.
Right: Octagonal corked marked "INK": $10.
Far right: Early molded type: $7.

Early commercial inks.
Left: Sanford's: $8.
Center: Cobalt Carter's: $15.
Right: Possible insert for a larger well, bakelite stopper, 1 inch tall: $8.

Two styles of early Carter bottles.
Left: With cut lip. 1-1/16 inches: $8.
Right: Slightly smaller: $7.

Bakelite type plastics made their debut in the early years of the 20th century.
Left: A school desk well: $15.
Center: Mini well often used for unusual colors of ink: $10.
Right: A ribbed example of the roll-proof type: $7.

Three styles of well with hobnailed base.
Left: 1-1/8 inch cube: $10.
Center: 2 -1/4 inches high with unusual lid resembling Imperial Glass Candlewick, which may pin down all
wells with this type base: $75.
Right: Small cube with silver floral cap: $45.

Crystal glass all-in-one inkstand/penrest/holder. Manufactured by a number of companies in the 1930s. Few of these ingenious units survive with the ink container undamaged. This fine example has a depressed funnel gravity-flow reservoir atop the double dipping miniature wells on each side. These all-purpose desk accessories were the last holdout of an earlier age as fountain pens began to replace the dip pen in the mid 1930s. 9-1/2 inches long by 13 inches wide: $125.

CUT GLASS

Cut or wheel-cut glass wells and bottles are often of exquisite quality, and are highly desirable to collectors. Often these were designed as inserts to grace a metal stand. At the beginning of the twentieth century some stands were also made of glass.

Cut glass of the brilliant style belonging to Victorian types is quite desirable. It is easy to mistake a perfume bottle or other vanity item for an inkbottle. Collectors should consult books on those items to be certain they are not purchasing a cologne bottle, thinking it an inkwell. Size of aperture is often a giveaway here, the perfume or lotion bottle having a more narrow hole at the top. Splash cologne was not yet the style in the Victorian era.

Here again, the recognizable work of famed glass producers may sometimes identify the maker of a given item.

Cut crystal well of 1890s "Brilliant" type lead crystal. 4 inches: $80.

SHELL

Inkwells of natural seashell were often produced for the earliest influx of tourist trade in England and the northeastern New England states. Souvenirs of trips to seacoasts, they were a reminder of a grand holiday. Many are marked with a city name, such as "Marblehead, Mass," but few have a maker's mark. They mainly were products of cottage industries where an individual's income was supplemented by gluing these shell inkwells and stands together by lamplight. The wells were generally sold through souvenir stores.

Shell wells were usually built around a larger shell, and then decorated with smaller shells.

Others were made of chalk or wood and covered with small shells and coral bits. A small glass vial was inserted that held only a teaspoon of ink. Mother-of-pearl wells are among the most expensive due to the loveliness of the material, and its appeal to European buyers. Large natural shells that have lost their dark, rough exterior are difficult to locate, and the use of such a shell or even a large insert will raise the price dramatically.

Finding any kind of maker's mark is so rare as to be quite exceptional, although there are sometimes clues supplied by the type of shell used, as to whether they were produced in the U.S. or across the Atlantic's waters.

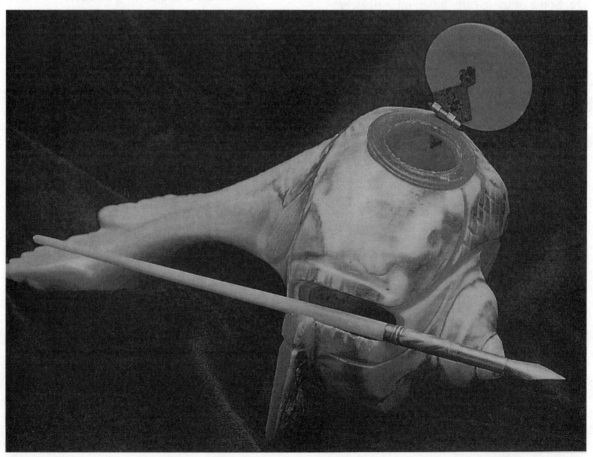

Pearl shell carved into a fish with small glass ink insert in head. Steel tipped pen in mouth. Shell inkwell: $190, pen: $60.

CHAPTER 3

INKWELL DESIGNS AND MOTIFS

TRAVEL WELLS

Before the advent of the fountain pen, which carried its own ink supply, a convenient holder for carrying ink while travelling was necessary. Most travel wells were made of wood and had a glass liner –more practical than a glass well alone that would have been more prone to breakage. Some of these early travel inkwells were produced in a thin, veneer-like treatment which was either press-fitted to hold it closed, or given a few "threads" after threading was invented to hold the top tightly. A patent was taken for several such wells as early as the 1830s. Soldiers on both sides of the Civil War conflict carried wells of this variety. One type involved a small metal spring in the base of the container that pushed a small glass ink vial upwards when the top was released. This raised it to a usable level and also had the advantage of allowing the user to see the level of the ink as he was using it.

Examples of these wells are found infrequently but now and then turn up at estate auctions involving several generations of a family.

BRUSH WELLS

Brush wells, which originated as long as 4000 years ago, feature very slim, narrow, deep receptacles. These wells were prevalent in the Middle East and Asia, where the use of writing reeds and brushes was more popular. Brush wells may be primitive or very well made, and some are nicely decorated and attractive. Brush wells may also hold smaller holes around the circumfer-

Travel wells had hinged tops and often had an extra lift cap to help prevent ink from leaking. Examples such as these range from $35 to $95, more if there is a name carved in the bottom.

ence, as brush reeds used for writing were quite narrow. It was common to find the reed alongside these holes, or lying flat to protect these fragile, shaped ends from bruising. Due to lack of recognition, collectors often overlook these brush wells.

When feathers began to be widely used, quill holes for these tools had to be built into the inkwell. Quill holes of slightly larger diameter are noted in wells of a later period and may reveal the fact that a given inkwell is not quite as old as a brush well. But it is not unimpeachable evidence, because the popularity of brushes and even reeds persisted in the Near East and Asia, even into quite recent times. Overlooked, but not without value, they are unusual reminders of our Eastern past.

ARTS AND CRAFTS

The Arts and Crafts Movement, which was influential during the late nineteenth and early twentieth centuries, was started in reaction to mass production brought on by industrialization.

Arts and Crafts practitioners emphasized hand craftsmanship and good quality. The style is sometimes referred to as "mission" or "craftsman" style. The use of simple forms and the crafting of utilitarian objects characterized the movement.

In America especially, the Arts and Crafts period replaced the use of wood for the most part, although some of these craftsmen did use the material. In the later years of the movement the use of wood declined and a variety of metals and ceramics took its place. Arts and Crafts wells of this period are highly sought.

Detail of owl with stylized "batwings" from photo below.

Late Victorian owl hinge-backed inkstand with stylized owl in medium relief. 5 inches by 9-1/2 inches in bronze with triple pen-rest. The hammered metal work and stylized representation were very characteristic of the Arts and Crafts period: $300.

A delightfully different set, obviously influenced by the Arts & Crafts period, this three piece group is cream-glazed pottery, with carved wood tops on both truncated-pyramid wells. The curve of the rocker blotter is almost humorous in its exaggeration: $205.

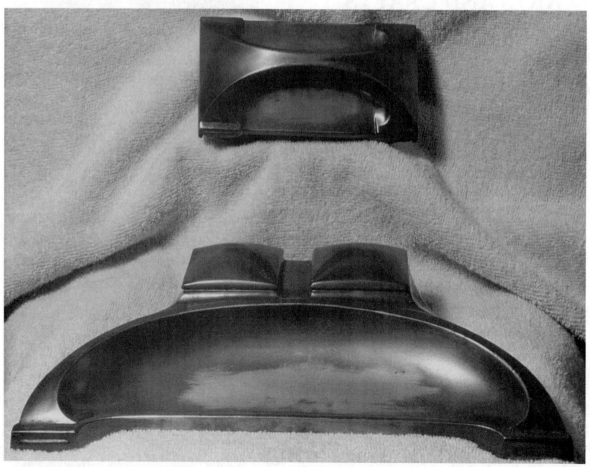

14 inch double copper bronze well and rocker blotter shows simple lines of the Arts & Crafts style. Very heavy: $220 set. Inkwell: $190, rocker blotter: $45-$50.

Group of three wells of the handmade Amish or Shaker type. Primitive in appearance, they are reminiscent of the Arts and Crafts Movement, which inspired them. Figures may be carved, hand-molded, or of fired clay.
Rear: Elephant with tusks, hinge-back single insert: $110.
Left: Dog with cap: $75.
Right: Carved elephant with rough shaping: $65.

Arts and Crafts style has often been compared to the simple designs of the Shaker and Amish communities. It was in these communities that almost the last of the wooden desk accessories was created to hold ink. Primitive and highly stylized in design, these wells are so deceptively simple they look as if a child could have created them. Widely carved from large or yellow pine, which were readily available and easy to work, they feature sharply angled carving in the round, and little or no realism in animal shapes. These are referred to as "animal cracker" inkwells, and are eagerly sought for and prized by many inkwell collectors.

FIGURAL WELLS

Figural inkwells and stands which were formed into animal or human shapes have a much shorter history, with a few rare exceptions dating from the Renaissance and beyond. Some of the earliest were carved from wood in the shape of a favorite animal, or modeled in clays to depict a figure from classical mythology or imagination. Figural wells were uncommon in any age, and so are difficult to find, and correspondingly unique as collectibles. It is very hard to locate duplicates of any figural inkwell.

An unusual shape keynotes both pieces of this set. Of dark bronze the Arts and Crafts styling is charming: $100-$125 set.

A good portion of those available are from the years 1700 to 1850 when the porcelain industry in France and Italy began to yield some prime examples of decorative figured wells. By the Napoleonic years, the trend was well established.

Animals

Animals comprise the largest number of figurals, and can be found in amazing variety, from hand carved German bears to pot-metal saddled camels, to dainty porcelain maidens gracing a gold-trimmed chariot.

Bengal tiger bares his teeth to guard an insert concealed behind his hinge-back face. A fine example with good paint: $450.

47

This elegant inkstand depicts a panther sculpted in exquisite detail in polished bronze. This large inkstand is a perfect reflection of the popular naturalistic style, which bridged the Art Nouveau and Art Deco influences. 7 inches by 13 inches: $850-$1000.

One popular group of wells includes the boldly modeled heads of dogs, bears, and even a Bengal tiger or two, whose upper cranium lifts backward to conceal the insert lurking behind the animal's muzzle. No marking is usually found on these wells, and they are usually made of hand painted metals, suggesting an origin in central Europe. The modeling is often heavy and

Note exquisite detailing of fur and stylized acorn cap on this wood inkstand. Some of these inkstands even include bear-tracks for additional realism: $300.

crude, indicating the use of a lost-wax molding method. Some of these wells are set with glass eyes while others are painted.

Bears are often the basic motif of Swiss-made wells. Many of these depict common European forest bears, some portrayed in natural settings of trees, stumps, and ravines. A few include the bear's actual tracks carved in the surface of the well, adding even more interest to the piece.

Glass eyes were sometimes added for additional realism, although this usage later became more popular in bears and animals carved for export and less for personal use. This tradition perhaps arose in Germany, and small dolls also were given glass eyes. Later the use continued in the turn of the century craze for the Teddy Bear, and the glass eye is still seen in this format.

Some of these early wells are so realistic that the fur, especially on the bear, is so detailed that

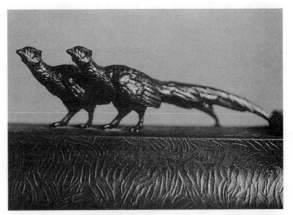

Detail of peacock-type birds on bronze inkwell. Late 1800s.

it looks almost soft to the touch. A bird's feathers might resemble the actual wing and tail feathers, rather than just a representation.

Woods used for inkwells ranged from oak to beech to linden, depending on the area and types

Rare in figural form, this floral well shows high relief wild flowers and a butterfly motif on the pen tray, with attached garden urn with hinge-backed white porcelain insert. The butterfly thumb-push is beautifully executed. 1880s: $275-$310.

This tiny gem, only 1-1/8 inches tall, is a child's well with delicate foliage and detailing on the stump, which is a hinge-back with a glass insert. The fawn is less detailed. Possible 1800s French early Nouveau style: $325.

A most unusual well from Germany, featuring a deer and foliage in relief on the green sponge-enameled surface. An elk-like addition in the rear might hold a pen on the antlers, but insecurely. A hinge-back lid conceals glass insert: $130.

Another of the mystery stands that features a puzzling large container with a smaller insert for ink. The deer-like creature provides a pen-rest for this interesting mid-1800s piece. The larger stump may have had a cover, and would have held wax or nibs. Poured light bronze 9 inches by 4 inches: $150.

Two of many camel styles so popular in the early 1920s following the opening of Tutankkomen's tomb in Egypt. On the left, a wooden "brush" well with narrow glass insert under saddle: $120. On the right a painted model in pot metal. The saddle hinges to conceal glass insert: $135-$145.

of available trees. Oak, being much harder and more difficult to carve, is consequently more rare. Oak will resist scratches and chips under normal usage for centuries. Oak was later used for a base upon which to add containers for ink.

Few price guides mention any type of wood or decorative style, probably because the information came from a buyer or seller to whom wood is wood, whether the hardest of ash or the softest of white pine. A few pieces are seen in veneer, but never so identified. Oak, cherry, rosewood and other such highly decorative woods are consequently much more expensive

and more highly prized by the true connoisseur of early or primitive inkwells, especially in the animal category.

Mediterranean countries and desert principalities tended to utilize olivewood, rosewood, and cedar, especially in the older wells. Some of these wells are highly decorative, too, and a common motif is the omnipresent camel. As it is much more likely that a brush or a shaped reed would be used in these desert areas than a metal pen point which might rust, some of these wells contain a deep and narrow ink container.

Art Nouveau

Flowing curved lines and highly ornamental designs characterized Art Nouveau, a decorative

Detail of owl atop bronze inkstand. Early twentieth century.

Detail of panther on bronze inkwell done in the Naturalistic style popular at the end of the nineteenth and beginning of the twentieth century.

The flowing hair of this Indian maiden is characteristic of the Art Nouveau style: $350.

Whimsical silver inkstand with dog biting one end of a newspaper "The Latest News", dated May 1, 1881: $250.

Unusual Art Nouveau stand with butterfly of very thin metal as pen-rest backing a typical floral tray with ramped crystal well: $140-160.

Detail of dog with newspaper from photo above.

art style popular at the end of the nineteenth and beginning of the twentieth centuries. The era of Art Nouveau is rich in delectable figurals, from girls with flowing hair to bronze lovebirds atop a vine-wreathed double inkstand of gleaming bronze crafted in Paris.

During this period, the great Louis Comfort Tiffany created some of his most beautiful desk sets that included inkwells of dazzling beauty. Working in relief, his patterns echoed nature's sweeping curves and flowering profusion. Some of these inkwells are a foot in height, covered

with the loveliest of bronze iris, while others are covered with the tracery of spider web or pine needles. One type of set was made in golden lace, inset with jewels, and looking like it might be found on the desk of a princess of the realm. It is from this period, 1870-1915, that the largest group of figural wells and stands has come, as other makers in America and on the Continent strove to equal the splendor of the Tiffany Studios.

Even Victorian humor may be reflected in inkwells from the period, including a naughty dog tearing at an unrolled newspaper, or a kitten with claws imbedded in a ball of yarn.

Because of the tendency of ink to discolor any item lacking an impermeable surface, most

A fine example of a popular Mid-Victorian theme, the lady forlorn waits by a fence. This small 4 inch by 5 inch piece is hinge-backed and contains a single insert: $185.

This naturalistic style inkstand in a bronze alloy features fine foliage detail and a stick designed to be used as a pen rest. Well has a hinge back and a rare white glass insert: $195-$210.

Classical full figured female in romantic pose made of unknown alloy. A single glass insert is concealed beneath the figure: 5-1/2 inches high by 6 inches long: $90.

Heavy bronze Art Nouveau angel, 14 inches wide. Extremely stylized, the well seems to flow up from between the angel's wings as an afterthought. The heavy curves and styling of the wings is distinctive, and angels are unusual in inkstands. This may have been a special design for a church. Hinge-back contains a single well insert: $250-$285.

Gleaming bronze Art Nouveau-style lady in the French mode is 6 inches high by 5 inches wide. The foliate designs on the under-plate culminate in a loose-lid formed of one single leaf in high molding. Her draped sash forms a pen-rest, then flows down into the under-plate. Note back portion is hinged to base, feet are pierced and clean: $400.

Warning: *This inkstand is being reproduced in brass. Detailing is NOT sharp and the piercing on feet may contain mold flanges and be almost closed. Repro values are less than $75 and the leaf insert lid is often absent.*

figural wells conceal glass or pottery inserts to keep the inks liquid and under control. Because the inserts were so easily broken, they are frequently missing in figurals. Missing inserts may be pirated from cheaper or broken wells, and some of these are now appearing as part of modern reproductions of brass inkwells coming from the Orient.

Tiffany

Naturally, the products of this great artistic and design house are in a class of their own, most wanted and desired by the collector, perhaps not so much for their styling as for their potential value which seems to appreciate by one hundred percent every few years. This is unfortunate but true. Louis Comfort Tiffany used whichever materials he found interesting without reference to their value. His art glass is of unparalleled excellence, and his metals range from vermeil to bronze, iron to gold, and include examples of extreme Art Nouveau styling to medieval shapes and designs. The iris and the dragonfly were great favorites of his and are found in use as part of his desk pieces as well as his jewelry.

One of the most overlooked of Tiffany categories is his inspired pine needle collection which features silvered metal filigree over green or amber Tiffany art glass. This style has often been considered less desirable to collectors than his spider web series. For Tiffany, however, the patterns of nature depicted by the pine tree were

1880s Venetian flower-bedecked gondola with hinge-back top concealing two white porcelain inserts. High relief design in heavy bronze. 9-1/2 inches: $425-$450.

just as lovely in spatial elegance as was the creation of the lowly spider. Over a dozen pieces comprised the pine-needle desk set, including inkwells, desk box, glass-handled paper knife, pen trays, and photograph frame. Prices of these items have climbed from $1,000 for a five-piece set of this pattern to $600 and more for each individual piece of the extensive set as collectors begin to discover their elusive and stylistic charm.

One of the most unusual pieces made by Louis Comfort Tiffany was a baronial inkstand. Early examples of this piece were marked with his personal stamp. After the large stand had shown its durability as a production item, it was given the Tiffany Studios mark. More than eleven inches in height and eight inches to a side, the piece tapers almost like a bronze volcano as it rises from a heavy base. Deeply detailed iris blooms and leaves adorn the piece on all four faces.

Tiffany products are at the top of the price spectrum and show no signs of abating in either collector interest or price. Those, which are fashioned of metal and glass, or inset with jewels of glass or actual gems, are among the priciest and most desirable. It is almost impossible to find a Tiffany piece which is not stamped with his initials or the company stamp, except for the rare instance in which a piece did not reach the stage in which it was offered for sale to the public. A trial piece or a discarded design which never saw production may have been spirited out of the master's studio and sold by someone else. Tiffany styling is almost uniquely recognizable, however, and can be identified by most upon sight. Pieces made by him, as special gifts to family or friends will, almost without exception, carry his mark.

ART DECO & MODERN

Art Deco, the prevalent style in the 1920s and 1930s, emphasized geometric shapes, an influence of Cubism. Lines were much more simplified in Art Deco designs, a reaction to the highly

Light and shadow are deceptive on this Bradley & Hubbard piece, restful to the eye. Note the simple clean lines of the Art Deco styling. The hinge-back covers a white insert: $325-$350.

ornate style of the Victorian and Art Nouveau periods.

Inkwells of this period may be of the cubed-off style, which was available until the late 1930s. The popularity of refillable fountain pens and filling bottles produced by inkmakers shoved the inkwell out of existence almost completely.

On a wafer of fired clay, this unusual piece is of Bakelite studded with ivory. 6 inches in diameter, a most striking Deco piece: $85.

Trio of gravity wells shows sleek styling of Art Deco period. Some of these wells were imprinted with advertising: $50-$75.

Some glass wells of this time are of the type which feature a heavy glass base with extra

Paperweight of what is variously called "composition" or "papier mâché" featuring the 1939 World's Fair Trylon and Perisphere — the epitome of Deco Styling: $35-$45.

pieces sitting upon molded holders in the felt-bottomed base. Some are round balls, which swivel in a 360-degree range, so that more than one person could draw ink from the well, or the opening could be pointed up and away to avoid spillage.

The collector will find that the largest group of available inkwells is of glass, and a few hours study will acquaint him or her with styles and vintages to which they belong. Some Art Deco style inkwells were also produced in metals. However, these wells tended to be made of tin, aluminum, or pot metal, and very few have survived.

ARCHITECTURAL

Many makers of inkstands used an architectural theme, molding their productions into the form of houses, cottages, cathedrals, and other buildings. The first of these were purely an art form, with no particular building in mind. They were often of simple clays or of wood, with or without an ink cup or container inside. Some with hinged lids made to conceal a single or double ink container set were of fantasy cottages, chalets, and even water-wheeled mills.

Folksy and often colorful, this type of well may form the basis of a fascinating side collec-

Log cabin with rustic look. Probably American but could be from Europe. Hinge-back roof exposes white glass well insert: $85.

56

tion. In a collection of miniature houses, such inkwells may provide an added accent of interest.

With the invention of tourism after the Middle Ages, this architectural bent advanced into the making of ink containers specifically mod-

eled from local buildings or famous attractions designed as keepsakes for the visiting public. Most popular were large churches and castles.

Tourism was apparently alive and well in the earlier days of the nineteenth century, as many

Sterling silver log cabin – an odd choice of material for the subject. Entire roof hinges back to reveal two white glass inserts: $180.

French inkstand with Napoleonic eagle buildings are portrayed in most of these which are of a style popular in Napoleon II's, France: $275-$325.

Detail of eagle from Napoleonic stand above.

wells are found in the form of monuments and triumphal arches of London and Paris. Mostly formed of pot metal, the ink cup sits concealed behind the architectural feature, or in some cases, has become a double well on each side of the central monument. Some few of these are bronze, silver, gilt, or tin, and were made in the early and mid-1800s in France, England, and even Spain.

Many of this type of inkstand were produced in or for the French and include such edifices as the Arc de Triomphe. Rare Statue of Liberty wells are sometimes encountered in Europe, less often in America. Most architectural wells and stands have been made of wood, bronze, or pot metal. There is hot interest amongst modern collectors in this special group of wells. Unfortunately, the U.S. seems to have fewer of these than are common in European countries.

Group of architectural model inkwells.
Left: From England, models of what appear to be parliamentary buildings, double wells, small: $70-80 each.
Center: Notre Dame full-form model on double inkwell stand. Period 1880s: $150 each.
Right: Grecian temple with dome, resembles a building in Jerusalem. Always hinge-back: $75 each.

CHAPTER 4

THE HISTORY OF PENS

Quill Pens

Just who first fashioned a feather into a pen is not known, but early references to quills are found in writings dating to about 550 AD. Made from the wing feathers of geese, quills had to be plucked from live birds, treated with heat, and shaped with a knife. The shaft of the feather was carved into a very sharp nib point, and the base of the shaft was slit. Through this slit, ink was drawn up into the shaft of the pen. The hollow shaft would hold the ink until light pressure was applied to the pen. Eventually, quill pens were widely used, fostering a considerable trade in geese. The feathers of swans and crows were also used as pens. Quills were not without drawbacks, however. They were expensive, troublesome, apt to break, and required that every writer also be a skillful pen mender.

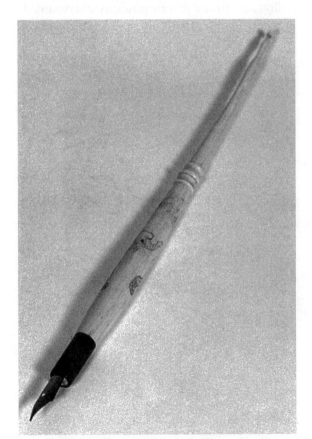

Carved ivory "pen-holder". "Pen" refers to only the writing tip, which can be replaced: $400.

Steel Pens

It is no surprise that early attempts were made to fashion pens from sheet steel. The first steel pen was a one-piece nib and holder. A sheet of steel was rolled into a tube with one end shaped to a point with the joining edges forming the slit. Later, improved pen points were cut from sheet steel, rounded, slit, ground, and tempered. The invention of the steel pen cannot be credited exclusively to one person, as there were many experimenters in the field. All contributed to the steel nib's final form.

Samuel Harrison is reputed to have made the first metal pens in England, and James Perry first advertised the new pen for sale. However, it is possible that France should be credited with the innovation; history records the manufacture of steel pens at Aix-la-Chapelle in 1748. "You will hardly tell by what you see that I wrote with a steel pen," wrote English biographer and lawyer Roger North to a friend. "It is a device came out of France, and when they get the knack of making them exactly, I do not doubt that the government of the goose quill will be at an end."

Early steel pens had little flexibility. To overcome this defect, the first American steel pens, made by Peregrine Williamson of Baltimore in the later half of the 1700s, featured two side slits. Until 1822 the manufacture of steel pens was done mostly by hand. Hence they were expensive, lacked uniformity, and could only be produced in small quantities. But in that year, James Gillott of Birmingham, who had been a Sheffield steel-worker, invented the steel pen press. This machine stamped out steel pens in huge numbers at little cost. Gillott later adapted machinery for other operations such as cutting, slitting, and bending. He introduced improvements in the hardening and tempering processes as well, and finally produced a steel pen equal to those we use today.

Interestingly, pen sizes were still tied to the feathers that they replaced. One asked for a crow point for bookkeeping or ledger work, a swan point for calligraphic work, and a quill for everyday writing. Women often preferred crow points because they produced clear fine lines, ideal for small writing. They had no holder other than an actual crow's feather, which they fit perfectly!

The early attitude of schoolmasters toward steel pens was less than positive. Nineteenth-century English author George Sala once wrote, "…when I went to school in Paris [ca. 1850] it was one of the highest crimes to be found in possession of a plume de fer! The steel pen was inflexibly banished as an abominable thing from our scholastic precincts."

Steel pens have been made and still are made in many different countries. Birmingham, England, where Sir Joseph Mason and Joseph Gillott set up their first factories, is still regarded as the historic center of the world's steel pen

Brass cherub is a single penholder on its own base. Cherub: $80, pen: $40.

Metal bear on folded brass is holder for a single dip pen. Holder and pen: $30 each.

An advertisement from 1910 espouses the virtues of Spencerian Steel Pens. "Spencerian" also referred to a style of slanted hand-writing popular in the late nineteenth and early twentieth centuries. Cosmopolitan Magazine ad page: $1.

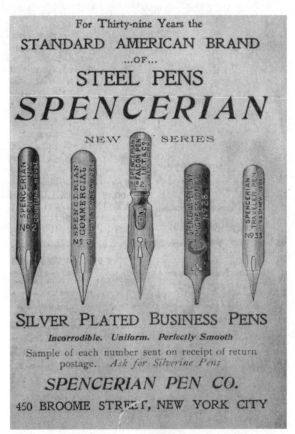

Back cover magazine ad showing Spencerian steel pens. Page: $1.50. Pens $1-$2 each.

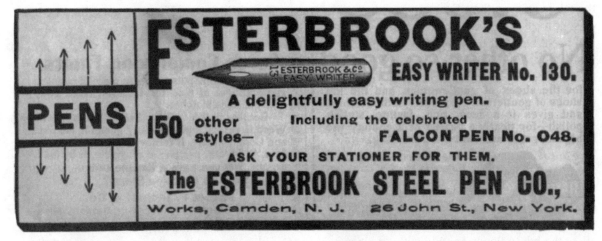

This 1899 advertisement for Esterbrook's features their "easy writer" pen. Munsey's Magazine ad page: $1.

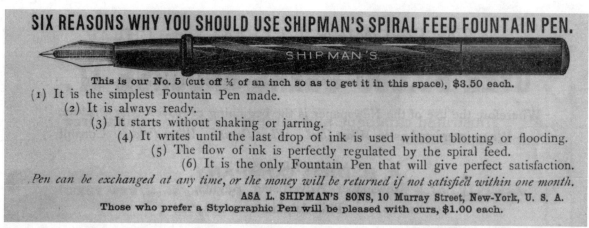

SIX REASONS WHY YOU SHOULD USE SHIPMAN'S SPIRAL FEED FOUNTAIN PEN.

SHIPMAN'S

This is our No. 5 (cut off ¼ of an inch so as to get it in this space), $3.50 each.

(1) It is the simplest Fountain Pen made.

(2) It is always ready.

(3) It starts without shaking or jarring.

(4) It writes until the last drop of ink is used without blotting or flooding.

(5) The flow of ink is perfectly regulated by the spiral feed.

(6) It is the only Fountain Pen that will give perfect satisfaction.

Pen can be exchanged at any time, or the money will be returned if not satisfied within one month.

ASA L. SHIPMAN'S SONS, 10 Murray Street, New-York, U. S. A.

Those who prefer a Stylographic Pen will be pleased with ours, $1.00 each.

This 1892 advertisement shows an early fountain pen, made by the Shipman Company. Many small pen-makers abounded in the early years of the fountain pen. Century Magazine ad:$1.25.

trade. Over a thousand different types of steel pen nibs are still on the market. Prices range from less than a dollar for simple types to several dollars for the more intricate styles. The nibs are used for all kinds of writing, calligraphy, drawing, and lithography work.

Fountain Pens

With the commercial production of fountain pens in the 1880s, the steel dip pen went into decline. L.E. Waterman invented the first practical fountain pen in 1884. His design was practical because it could reliably hold ink and release the ink in an even flow. Fountain pens had existed for more than 100 years, but no design had been reliable for widespread commercial production. Holding its own ink supply, the fountain pen eliminated the messy and nearly constant dipping of the pen in an inkwell.

Fountain pens have three main components: the reservoir, the feed mechanism, and the nib. The reservoir, usually a rubber sac in early models, holds the ink. The most important quality in the reservoir is that it be leak-proof. The feed mechanism, called a feed-bar, channels the ink from the reservoir to the nib. The feed-bar must allow the ink to flow smoothly without separating. Waterman's design added an air hole in the nib, along with three grooves in the feed mechanism. These grooves allowed the ink to flow

more readily to the nib than had earlier designs. The nib, usually made of gold, has an air-hole and a slit to allow the ink to travel to the tip. Gold became the metal of choice for nibs as it was more malleable than steel, allowing for finer writing styles. Gold was also a practical choice as it did not corrode and rust as steel did. However, because gold is such a soft metal, the nibs on early fountain pens wore down very quickly. A small pellet or ball was soon added, usually made of either iridium or beryllium, to keep the nib from wearing down. Both of these metals are very strong and resistant to corrosion, making them ideal for pen nibs.

The earliest fountain pens were filled with an eyedropper, a method that proved nearly as messy as dipping. By the early 1900s, several mechanisms were developed that allowed ink to be drawn up directly into the pen. The most prevalent design was the lever filler. An external lever, when lifted, depressed the rubber reservoir sac. The nib was then placed in the inkbottle or well, and the lever released. With the release of pressure, ink was drawn up through the nib and feed-bar into the reservoir.

Several designs for lever filling mechanisms were patented around the turn of the century. Conklin invented the crescent filler in 1897. His design is generally considered the first self-filling mechanism for fountain pens. A crescent shaped disc protruded from the side of the Conklin pen.

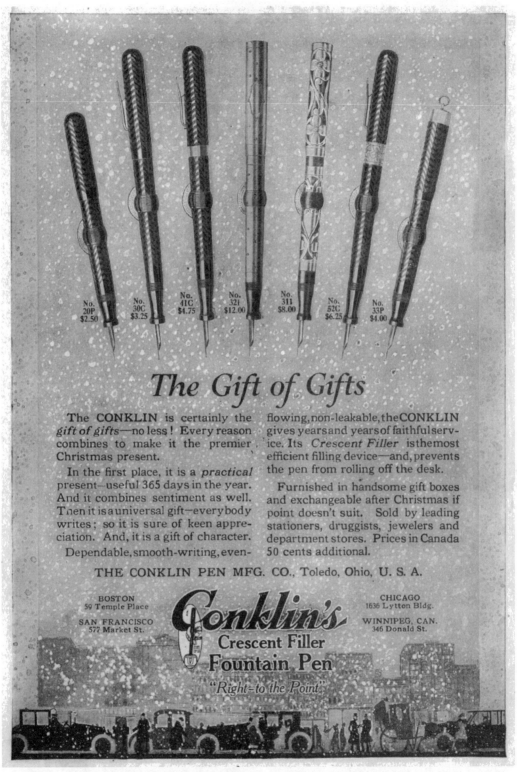

Magazine page from 1919 featuring the current styles and models of Conklin hard black rubber or trimmed pens. In mint condition, these pens would range from $50 to $200 for the two gold-plated models in the center. Conklin was one of the big makers, and featured a most interesting filling mechanism. Atlantic Monthly *ad page: $2.50.*

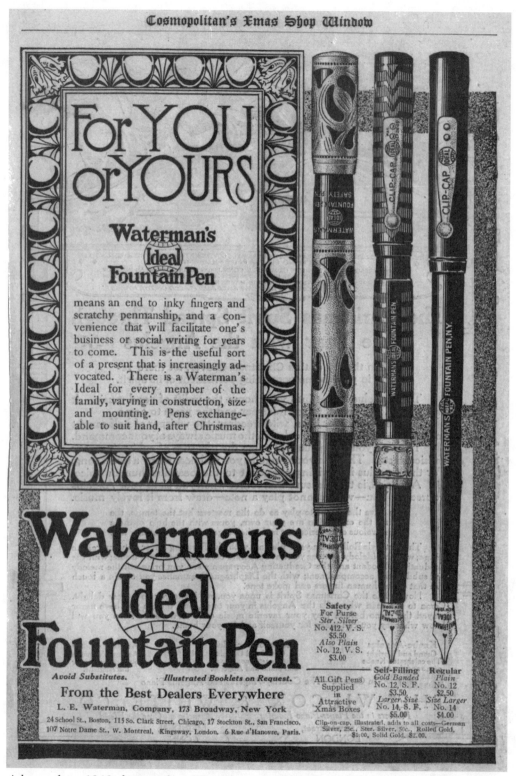

Ad page from 1913 showing three Waterman pens. The short capped pen to left is a "safety" pen whose nib could be retracted back into the barrel to protect the soft gold tip. The pen in the center is a "self-filler" and the pen on the right is an "eye-dropper" filler. Cosmopolitan Magazine ad page:$4.50.

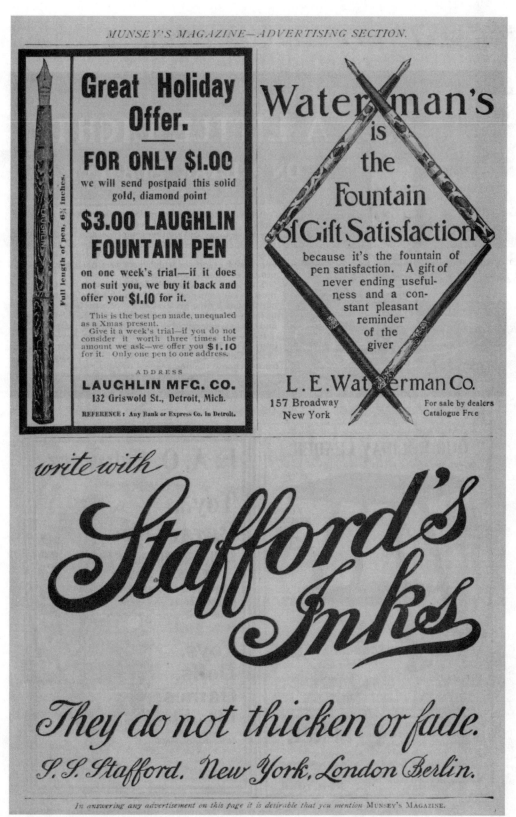

Munsey's Magazine *ad featuring Waterman and Laughlin fountain pens and Stafford Ink. The Laughlin pen appears to be of a mottled or marbled black rubber. Advertisement:$3.*

Another of the small pen-makers, D. W. Beaumel, is featured in this ad from 1897. Munsey's Magazine ad page: $2.

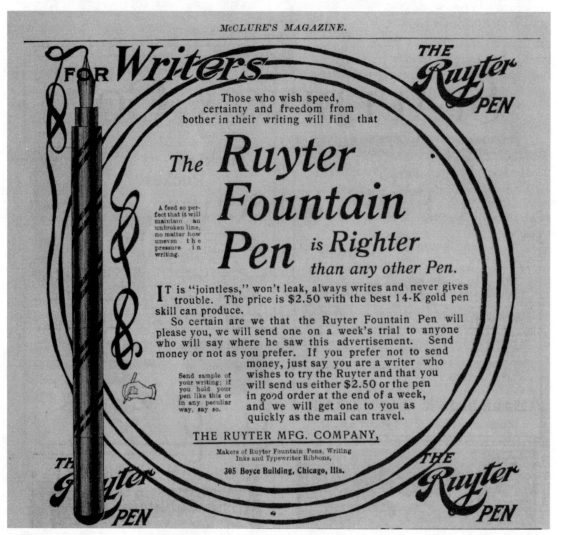

1899 Ruyter fountain pen ad. One is led to wonder how many pens the company lost through this promotion… McClure's Magazine ad:$2.

When unlocked and depressed, the disc would deflate the rubber reservoir sac and allow ink to enter the pen. In 1905, Parker patented the button filler system. An external button found on the end of the pen's barrel connected to a plate inside. When the button was depressed, the plate would deflate the rubber sac. A blind cap often concealed the button. Parker, however, did not start using this design in production until 1913. The lever filler was invented by Sheaffer in 1908 and became the most widely used design for the next forty years. The lever was located on the side of the pen and fit flush with the barrel when not in use. When lifted, the lever depressed the reservoir sac inside the pen.

The earliest commercially available fountain pens were fashioned of hard black rubber. Chasing or fine ridging was added to the hard rubber to improve the gripping surface, and often was formed in a wavy design that was the same on cap and barrel. This chasing became somewhat ornate on some special pens, and the manufacturer often added gold accents. Although pocket clips were not yet in supply, pens could be equipped with clips manufactured overseas if a purchaser desired one. These early gold accents are highly sought whether they are simple bands around the cap or barrel, or provided enough space for an engraver to add initials or a name to the pen. Some of these fine accents are solid

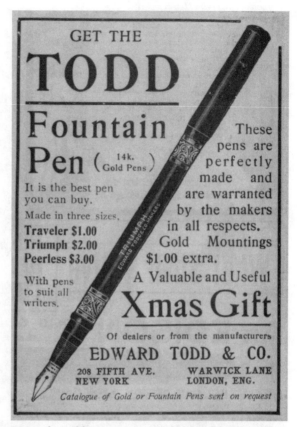

Note the gold mountings on this hard black rubber pen by the Edward Todd company. Todd made a fine pen! McClure's Magazine *ad from 1902:$1.*

An Edison Pen from 1902 featured a 14 karat gold pen point. McClure's Magazine *ad: $1.*

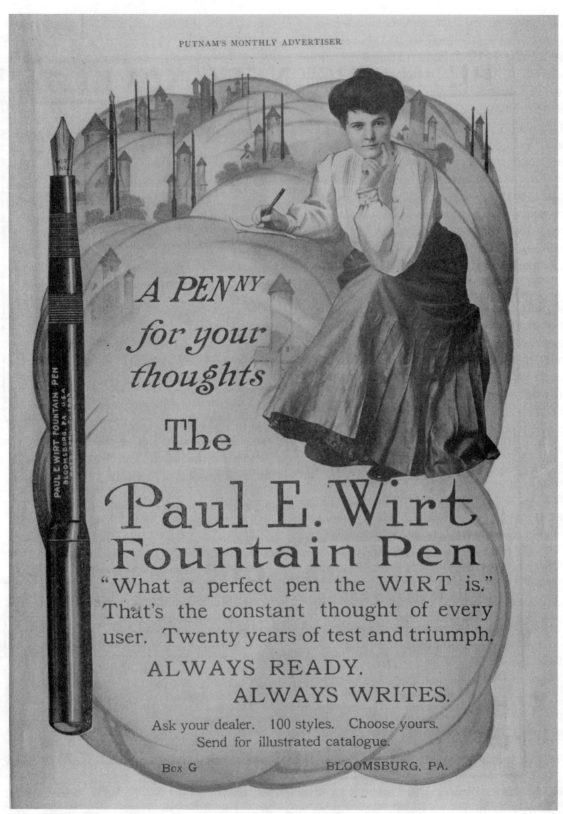

This 1906 ad features a Gibson girl surrounded by Maxfield Parrish type castles! The Wirt pen shown in the advertisement is quite plain by comparison. Putnam's Magazine ad:$1.

gold but most are gold plated on the better known pen-maker's products. Gold wash is common on lesser brands.

As these pens became more popular, their variety increased. Some were made very long to hold more ink in a slim width designed for stenographers using shorthand. They are in a special category of their own, usually made by Waterman. A sharp chasing and a nicely formed gold accent will add much to the value of an early pen. Most of these have the pen-maker's name on the side of the barrel, and many include the patent date as well.

It was not long before pens began to become popular with all classes of society, and in an effort to intrigue the more wealthy, they acquired a covering sheath of metal, either solidly formed or in a filigreed style. Stock gold,

gold-filled, or silver "lace" filigrees were added to hard black rubber pens as an enticement. The lacy openwork designs appealed mainly to women at first, but pen-makers soon added snake, tree-trunk, and Aztec designs to appeal to men. Although chasing and filigrees added style and class to fountain pens, they were still all produced in the somewhat somber black rubber.

Makers experimented with adding color, but most colorants tended to make the rubber hard and brittle. As the 1920s approached, red rubber began to be mixed into the black as a sales promotional device. Some very attractive treatments and styles of marbled, streaked, and swirled red and black pens were produced. Red hard rubber was not quite as sturdy as black so only a few makers produced models made only of red. Few of these were given the wavy chasing designs, as

Hull fountain pen with very attractive chased design in the black rubber. 1898 McClure's Magazine *ad page:$1.*

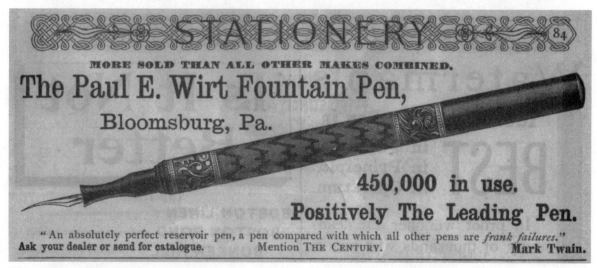

This 1892 ad from Century Magazine *features a very attractive Wirt fountain pen with chasing and gold filigree. Ad page: $1.*

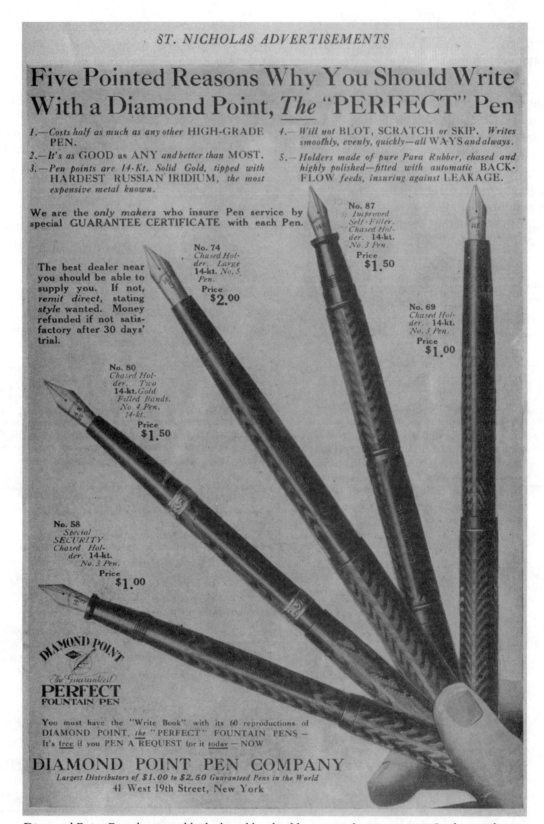

Diamond Point Pens began as black chased hard rubber pens of various types. In this condition, these pens would be worth $20-$50 today. St. Nicholas Magazine ad from 1913: $1.25.

this tended to weaken the rubber even more. In the early Twenties, the Parker Pen Company broke the tradition of using hard black rubber entirely, and conquered the market with their new Big Red Duofold pen, which at $7.00 was usually half the weekly wage for a working man. The popularity of Parker's red pen spurred other makers to produce colorful pens of their own.

Sheaffer was the first to introduce colorful plastic pens in 1924. Pens had been made of celluloid and casein, but were ivory or translucent in color. These materials were also quite brittle and often did not hold up to the rigors demanded of many fountain pens. In the early 1920s, DuPont developed a new "unbreakable" celluloid called pyroxylene. Of course, this new plas-

Group of colorful, but generally inexpensive fountain pens of lesser makers.
Left: Forefront; Swallow pen in marbled plastic: $95.
Middle: Moore pen: $60.
Right: Sheaffer flat top: $75 and up depending on color.
The pens to the rear are generally in the $10-$20 range. Note the various patterns on these early plastic pens.

tic was not truly unbreakable, but it was much stronger and less brittle than earlier varieties of celluloid. This new substance also took colorants quite easily. Sheaffer called this substance "Radite" and began to turn out bright, eye-catching plastic pens. Parker, taking the lead from Sheaffer, quickly added colorful plastic pens to its Duofold line. During the 1920s and 1930s most pen-makers switched to the new plastics for their pens. By the early 1940s, the injection molding process had been developed, making production of plastic pens quicker than ever.

Ballpoint pens, invented in 1938 by Laszlo Biro, took the pen industry by storm much as the fountain pen had fifty years earlier. By the late 1940s, the ballpoint was quickly replacing the fountain pen as the writing instrument of choice. Not a beauty, ballpoint pens leaked, clogged, and were as bothersome as their fluid ink predecessors. They found their niche due to their very inexpensive price and the fact that if they acted up, they could be thrown away at no large loss.

Only artists, calligraphers, and a few curmudgeons, who were resistant to change from elegance to convenience, were unashamed to be

Steel nibbed pens:
Left: $20 black hard rubber.
Middle: $25 marbled.
Right: $35-40 oversize yellow.

Inkograph pens were popular with artists but not with the man on the street. An early variation of the ballpoint, these pens did not sell well. Today these pens would bring $40-$45 each. American Magazine *ad from 1926: $2.*

seen using a nibbed pen. "Those leaky old things," most said, "they're a messy nuisance." Everyone had a tale to tell of a shirt pocket drenched in non-removable ink, a spot on a suit , tie, or tablecloth, or a dry, empty pen which had prevented the writing of an important document.

Fountain pens, it seemed, were a dead issue for over thirty years. Probably hundreds of thousands were left lying forgotten in drawers, pitched into the "round file," bundled hurriedly into cigar boxes destined for dim basement shelves, or in a few cases, used as darts by some enterprising youngster. The fabled decades of elegance in writing were dead at last. The long lasting romance was over. Fountain pens were as unwanted and useless as Maxfield Parrish prints and Tiffany lamps...

RENAISSANCE AND REBIRTH

Toward the late 1970s only a handful of antique or jewelry shops might have held a single grubby, twisted, or broken fountain pen. These were only suffered to remain there by virtue of extremely large sizes, or a Victorian elegance of filigreed metal covering their apparent uselessness.

Even in the 1990s, most dealers or shop owners preferred to ignore them as a low-interest item, or one about which they knew little and could find out less. With the publication of *Collectible Fountain Pens* by Glenn Bowen, a price guide and index, a few more pens began to resurface.

Rebirth of American interest in old pens may have been begun, oddly, by a company whose distinctive styling, white-capped end and lordly sizes began to capture the interest of lawyers and globetrotting businessmen with multinational concerns.

Swiss company Mont Blanc, long continuing to produce fine writing instruments in the decades of death (1955-1985), began to make inroads amongst men to whom image was

important. Some of these bolder individuals rediscovered the potential of a fine writing instrument adorning an otherwise useless suit pocket bereft of its formerly fashionable handkerchief. Men, wary of jewelry other than a watch, tie-pin, or ring, found the former pocket-filling folded kerchief had lost its allure, but discovered that a strong masculine image could be enhanced by a high-style pen in the erstwhile nose-blower's place.

Almost with miraculous suddenness, the European maker Mont Blanc's products were being worn like badges of good taste in suits from off the peg to Armani. Most prevalent were those of the largest size and equivalent price. Everyone KNEW what you had paid for the pen projecting from your pocket, and oohs and aahs of inferiors added prestige to the mix.

Mont Blanc's distinctive white mountain emblem on the top of the cap helped galvanize the renaissance of the fountain pen in the 1980s.

But what about those older pens whose classic elegance had led them and their makers to world dominance in the years between the Great Wars? What of the forgotten gems of manufacturers such as Waterman, Conklin, and Parker? Where were these "oldies but goodies" now?

Like cooling lava from a dying volcano, some farsighted men in various places were beginning to take notice of old pens. After all, everyone who had the price could sport a big black Mont Blanc with its signature white tip and engraved gold nib. Prestige, like many other things, is made of many parts. If it conferred instant panache to sport a bulging foreign pen in ones suit or shirt pocket, what would be the effect of one of those fine old pens Grandpa had used with such finesse?

Glen Bowen and others were consulted and questioned about the availability, and reparability of old fountain pens. Almost alone on the scene, they were quickly pushed to a position of authority that must truly have amazed them with its rapidity and ferocity. The small, backroom-meeting Los Angeles Pen Club, conceived by such men as Dr. Bob Tefft, published a modest membership notice and were quickly over-

whelmed by "members at large" from every state of the union and many foreign countries, few of whom could attend club meetings.

This pen's resemblance to niello work insert with a faceted ruby, makes it unique in design. It is 5-1/2 inches in length, gold nibbed. The work of D.J. Kennedy and other designers heralded the dawning of a new era in pen-making history: $900 each and up. Courtesy D.J. Kennedy, Kennedy Art Studios, Chester, Illinois.

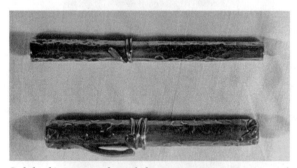

Solid silver examples of the artistic pen creations of D.J. Kennedy of Chester, IL. Kennedy was the first to craft unique new fountain pens and inkwells. He uses precious metals and gems to create fantastically different creations now carried exclusively by Nieman-Marcus.
Top: Hammered silver "snake" pens 5 inches: $500 each.
Bottom: Applied clip on thick sterling pen spiced with a copper "jewel" 1994: $650 each. Courtesy D.J. Kennedy.

Baroque clip pen with melting swirls of high relief. Gold nib, and piece of natural amber. This pen was created especially for author Ray Jaegers in 1993: $1500-$2000. Courtesy D.J. Kennedy.

CHAPTER 5

FOUNTAIN PEN MAKERS LARGE AND SMALL

During the heyday of the fountain pen, there were dozens of companies competing in the market place. Three of these companies largely dominated the field: Waterman, Parker, and Sheaffer. These three companies were largely responsible for many of the innovations in the fountain pen field.

WATERMAN

As the apocryphal story goes, insurance salesman L.E. Waterman was spurred to invent a reliable fountain pen when a reservoir pen he was using blotted and smeared an important contract. As a result, Waterman's client cancelled the contract and Waterman retired to invent a better pen. Whether this story is true or merely good advertising copy for the company

Waterman's pavilion in the Palace of Industry at the St. Louis World's Fair of 1904. Note the huge fountain pens at each of the four corners. Historic photos such as this are priceless.

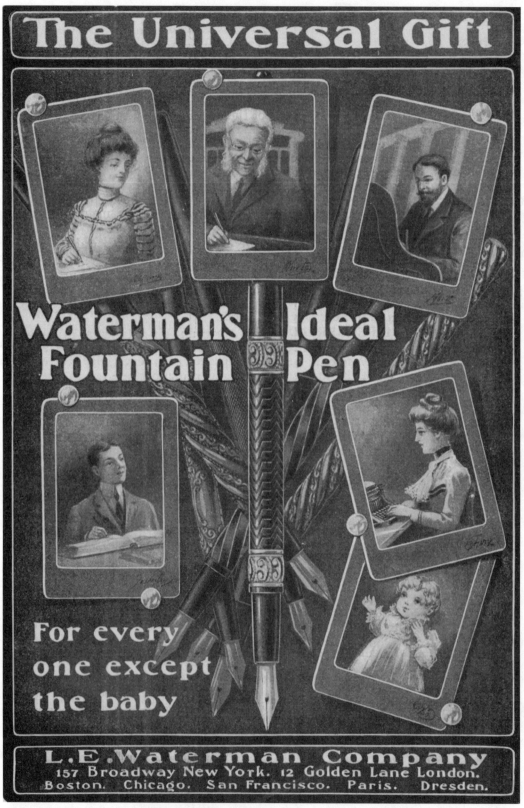

Fascinating 1902 ad featuring women as pen-users. Twist type pens in gold or silver valued at $150 and up. Advertisement: $5-$6.

An ad with double value as it features an airplane as well as fountain pen advertising. The sky-writing airplane of the 1920s was exciting and dangerous! Waterman pen in "woodgrain" pattern, most common in red and black, black and green less common, and black and blue most unusual. Pen ranges from $35 to more than $150. National Geographic advertising page from 1929: $4-$6.

Waterman ad from 1926 featuring pens made of red and black swirled hard rubber. Red rubber is more likely to crack, so these pens are harder to find than black rubber pens. Pen $125, pencil $75, set $195 and up, depending on size and condition. National Geographic *advertising page: $3-$5.*

Advertising page for Waterman's early hard rubber pens. The hard black rubber pen features a very intricate floral design. Century Magazine ad from 1893: $2.

Waterman went on to found, he did succeed in producing a more reliable pen.

Waterman obtained patents for his improvements in the early 1880s, and incorporated his company in 1888. Waterman's biggest innovation was the improved feed mechanism, which allowed ink to flow more freely from the reservoir to the nib. The Waterman "Ideal" fountain pen quickly became a best seller for the company. Like the majority of early fountain pens, the Ideal was made of hard black rubber and early models were filled with an eyedropper. Waterman's answer to the self-filling mechanism was the coin filler. A coin was pressed into a slot on the pen's barrel, which depressed the reservoir sac and allowed ink to be drawn up into the pen.

After L.E. Waterman's death in 1901, the company became more conservative and its main innovations were a response to the other industry leaders.

Parker Pens

George Safford Parker was granted a patent for an improved fountain pen design in 1889. In 1892 he started the Parker Pen Company in Janesville, Wisconsin. One of Parker's earliest innovations was the "Lucky Curve" ink feed system. Patented in 1894, this feed mechanism was designed to allow the ink to flow back into the reservoir when the pen was upright – as it would be when carried in a pocket. An improved Lucky Curve was patented in 1911 and remained the company's chief feed system for the next decade. A 1913 Parker advertisement explains the advantages of the Lucky Curve system:

Why does a pen write? Because the touch of the pen point to the paper creates Capillary Attraction – that curious force in Nature that makes sponges absorb, lamp wicks draw, etc., etc. This Capillary Attraction draws the ink from the pen point onto the paper.

Why does a fountain pen leak? Because when you set an ordinary fountain pen in your vest pocket, point up, all the ink does not run down into the reservoir below. Some stays up in the straight feed tube leading to the pen point. When your body heat – 98 degrees— reaches the air in the pen barrel, the air expands – rushes up through the inky feed tube – pushed the ink up and out around the pen point – messes the writing end of the pen – and blacks your fingers when you remove the cap. Now the Parker, unlike other fountain

1913 Parker Pen ad touting the company's "Lucky Curve" feed system which guided the last bit of ink up to the tip of the pen, or back down to the barrel when the pen was upright. The jack knife safety pen was a new model for Parker in 1913. Jack knife safety pen (left) $120, black rubber pen with chasing (center) $45 and up, black rubber pen with gold bands (right) $100 and up. Cosmopolitan Magazine ad page: $5.

Parker World War I military ad from Red Cross Magazine of June 1918. Note the aviator in typical helmet, goggles, and fur-collared jacket. Military pens often included a small compartment with ink pellets for troops to write in the field. Pens: $45 - $75. Advertisement: $3.50-$5.

pens, has a curved feed tube – the famous Parker Lucky Curve. The end of it touches the barrel wall. This touch creates Capillary Attraction, which draws all the ink down out of the feed tube when you turn pen up, and before the air expands.

Thus the thing that makes a pen write is the same thing that keeps the Parker Pen from leaking and smearing the fingers – to wit: Capillary Attraction.

In the early 1900s, Parker introduced gold filigree styles to their pen line. An important innovation on these pens was the taper on the inside of the outer cap. This design held the cap on more securely and helped prevent leaks.

Parker was also the first to introduce a safety screw-on cap on its Jack Knife model of 1912.

Although patented in 1905, Parker did not introduce their button filler until 1913. A button, concealed on the end of the barrel by a cap, was connected to a plate inside the barrel. When the button was depressed, the plate deflated the reservoir and allowed ink to enter the pen. Button mechanisms were found on most Parker pens until the vacumatic filler was introduced in the 1930s.

World War I spurred Parker to invent the "trench pen," for which the company was awarded a government contract in 1917. Instead of using liquid ink, the pen was designed to use ink pellets to which water was added. The pellets were easier and less messy for soldiers to

A Parker ad from World War I featuring pens with high clips to hide in a soldier's pocket and not gleam to catch the light. Jack knife pen (left) $45 and up, black rubber pen with elaborate decoration (right) $100 silver, $135 gold. 1917 Red Cross Magazine *ad page: $3-5.*

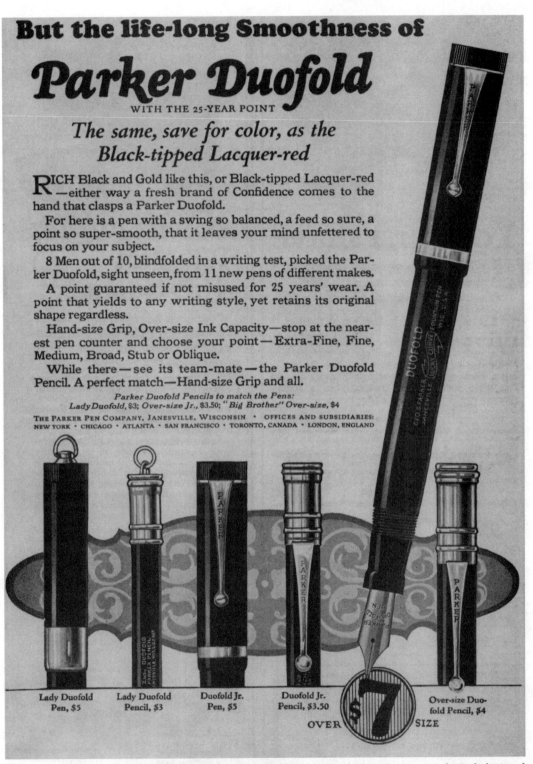

But the life-long Smoothness of

Parker Duofold

WITH THE 25-YEAR POINT

The same, save for color, as the Black-tipped Lacquer-red

RICH Black and Gold like this, or Black-tipped Lacquer-red —either way a fresh brand of Confidence comes to the hand that clasps a Parker Duofold.

For here is a pen with a swing so balanced, a feed so sure, a point so super-smooth, that it leaves your mind unfettered to focus on your subject.

8 Men out of 10, blindfolded in a writing test, picked the Parker Duofold, sight unseen, from 11 new pens of different makes.

A point guaranteed if not misused for 25 years' wear. A point that yields to any writing style, yet retains its original shape regardless.

Hand-size Grip, Over-size Ink Capacity—stop at the nearest pen counter and choose your point—Extra-Fine, Fine, Medium, Broad, Stub or Oblique.

While there—see its team-mate—the Parker Duofold Pencil. A perfect match—Hand-size Grip and all.

Parker Duofold Pencils to match the Pens:
Lady Duofold, $3; Over-size Jr., $3.50; "Big Brother" Over-size, $4

THE PARKER PEN COMPANY, JANESVILLE, WISCONSIN • OFFICES AND SUBSIDIARIES:
NEW YORK • CHICAGO • ATLANTA • SAN FRANCISCO • TORONTO, CANADA • LONDON, ENGLAND

Lady Duofold Pen, $5

Lady Duofold Pencil, $3

Duofold Jr. Pen, $5

Duofold Jr. Pencil, $3.50

OVER $7 SIZE

Over-size Duofold Pencil, $4

In the mid-1920s, hard black rubber was beginning to completely lose favor to early Bakelite and plastic. In this ad, Parker made a plea to the old-fashioned pen buyer. The Sr. Duofold would bring about $100 today, the Jr. size and ring-topped models less. In the 1920s, the ring-tops became known as "Lady Duofolds" as most men had stopped wearing watch chains. 1926 National Geographic ad page: $3.

The famous "Big Red" Duofold pens are featured in this ad from 1924. Atlantic Monthly *ad page: $3.*

"This Laminated Beauty is Rated by Students as the GRANDEST GRADUATION GIFT PEN" — says Ripley

Believe It or Not! by Ripley

I ASKED 4,445 STUDENTS Representing 21 Colleges "WHAT FOUNTAIN PEN WOULD YOU PREFER AS A GRADUATION GIFT?" AND 48.9% OF ALL WHO REPLIED—CHOSE PARKER! Parker led the second choice pen by 46.4%

Visible Ink Supply

102% More Ink

LESS THAN ACTUAL SIZE.

Holds 102% More Ink

RELIEF GLOBE BY RAND MC NALLY & COMPANY

Its Visible Column of Ink, like the gas gauge on a motor car, shows when to refill—and it carries enough to write a 12,000-word book!

A widespread inquiry among students was recently made by Ripley to aid friends and parents in selecting the Gift Pen that will gladden Youth the most. And he found an overwhelming preference for this revolutionary Parker Vacumatic.

One reason is that it eliminates 14 old-time pen parts, including the rubber ink sac—thus it holds 102% more ink *without increase in size!*

Its laminated style is wholly smart and exclusive—it is built up ring upon ring of shimmering Pearl and Jet, but the "Jet" becomes Transparent when held to the light, revealing the column of ink inside. This shows days ahead when it's running low—lets the user choose his own time to refill.

Its Platinum, Gold, and Iridium Point is included at the regular price, although 25% more costly to make

than a year ago, due to the higher prices of precious metals. It's as smooth as the bearing of a watch—doesn't scratch or drag, even under big-fisted pressure.

But be careful—don't confuse this sacless marvel with so-called vacuum fillers built with piston pumps and valves. The great Parker Vacumatic contains none of these—nothing that will fail to stand up in service. That's why Parker guarantees it mechanically perfect! Stop at any good department, stationery, jewelry, or drug store, and see this miracle writer demonstrated. The Parker Pen Company, Janesville, Wisconsin.

WRITES TWO WAYS

upper nib writes hair-line or extra fine or fine

Lower nib writes fine or medium or broad, etc.

WITHOUT ADJUSTMENT

Parker VACUMATIC

Over-Size, $10; Pencil, $2.50 — $7.50 — Other Vacumatic Styles, $5

To Make a Pen a Self-Cleaner use Parker Qu*ink*—a new discovery in writing ink. It contains a harmless, secret solvent that cleans a pen as it writes.

Parker introduced its new filling system, the Vacumatic, in the 1930s. Note the arrow logo on the pen clip. 1934 National Geographic ad page: $2.

carry in the field. Parker advertisements from 1918 offer ink tablets "for a soldier's 'kit' in place of fluid ink." Parker also touted the fact that "injury to self-filling mechanism does not put the Parker out of commission…it automatically changes from a self-filler to a non self-filler without interruption of service."

Parker introduced the Duofold line in 1920. Duofold pens were notable for their ink capacity, bold styling, neat and stylish clips, and the very efficient "duo-fold" ink feed. Begun in black hard rubber, the early models were quickly replaced by the orange-colored "Big Red" rubber pen in 1921. The adventurous George Parker advertised the flame-colored front-runner of the Duofold family by sending his orange-red airplane flying from one town to another With the introduction of more stable and less brittle plastics in the mid-1920s, Parker began making the Big Red model in plastic. On his fabled trip to the land of the ancient Mandarin culture, Parker encountered an exquisite vase of brilliant yellow porcelain. This vase inspired

the second color, a stunning yellow, for his burgeoning Duofold line. From perhaps the same exotic source, the legendary lapis blue was created, and crowned Parker's leap from ordinary hard rubber pens into the colorful rainbow popularity cycle of the giddy 1920s.

These pens were all button-fillers, and came in five different sizes, each one larger than the next. They can be readily identified by their flat tops, distinctive Parker clips, and the small black cap that hides the small button-filler at the rear. A find of a Duofold pen which still has its pen stand and its normal cap would be a bonanza for any general antiques dealer, as depending on color, the set might bring anywhere from $200, if orange-red, to $800 or more if lapis blue or mandarin yellow.

Parker showed continuing innovation in the 1930s with the introduction of the vacumatic filler. This new system worked by means of a plunger, which when tapped several times would expel air through the feed and draw up ink into

The Parker 51, the third revolution in pens, featured a "Space Age" hooded nib. The nib was still gold, but hidden inside the pen when not in use. This pen was the preferred men's gift of the 40s and 50s. Courtesy Ray and Helen Call.

the barrel. The entire barrel interior acted as the reservoir, allowing the pen to hold about twice the amount of ink of previous designs. As with the Duofold line, the vacumatic pens were boldly styled in plastic. Some featured a transparent window in the barrel so the user could see how much ink remained in the pen. Vacumatics are also notable for featuring the distinctive Parker arrow logo on their clips.

The Parker 51 was introduced in 1941, commemorating the 51st anniversary of the company. The 51 sold in such huge numbers that it is still readily encountered in almost any estate. The 51's distinctive design has a bullet shape, with only a tiny glint of the nib showing. During the 1930s Parker developed a new, fast-drying ink. However, due to the corrosive nature of this new ink, Parker could not use celluloid in its new pen. For this reason, the 51 was molded in a brand new plastic called "lucite" which was not corroded by the ink.

SHEAFFER

Walter A. Sheaffer, inventor of the lever filler, started the Sheaffer Pen Company in 1912 in Fort Madison, Iowa. The convenience of the lever filler quickly made Sheaffer a major competitor in the fountain pen industry.

In 1920 Sheaffer introduced its "Lifetime" pen point. Each Lifetime point was given a serial number and carried a lifetime guarantee from Sheaffer. Priced at $8.25, the Lifetime pens were more than double the price of Sheaffer's less expensive models and those of its competitors. Despite the steep price, the Lifetime line sold very well, and stayed in Sheaffer's lineup for several decades. A 1921 advertisement for the Lifetime pen was obviously pitched to the well-to-do businessman of the day:

Adopted by Men Who Write in Big Figures The 'LifeTime' SHEAFFER is the most important advancement in Fountain Pen manufacture since the original lever-filler, which was invented by W.A. SHEAFFER. It is larger than the ordi-

nary fountain pen and holds a much greater supply of ink.
Its extra heavy gold nib with indestructible iridium point writes with perfect smoothness and will stand the extra pressure necessary to make carbon copies – five, if necessary, just as easily as the hardest pencil.

Sheaffer again led the way in 1924 with the introduction of plastics to the fountain pen industry. Using a new plastic they labeled "Radite," Sheaffer's first plastic pens were in marbled green and black. Pens in bright Art Deco colors of the decade soon followed. These colorful pens, a welcome relief from the somber black rubber pens, were an instant hit. Other pen companies were soon producing their own plastic pens in a variety of colors.

Sheaffer assiduously avoided the word "ink" when referring to Skrip, calling it instead a "writing fluid." Introduced in the 1920s, Skrip is still produced today. Pictured here is a Sheaffer's master inkbottle used by teachers to fill student ink wells in desks. "The day we wrote with ink" is still a special memory for pre-1960s school children who remember it fondly. Ink with box: $40, if clean as in this example. Bottle alone: $25. Unusual colors (not blue-black): $30-$35 each.

The desk lamp and double pen stand pictured in this 1928 Sheaffer ad made a premier office gift. The white dot on the pen was Sheaffer's "Lifetime" logo. Desk set: $300 and up. Ad page: $3.00.

By the late 1940s, most of the big pen-makers were offering ball point pens along with their fountain pens. This Sheaffer ad from 1949 features two sets with the "Stratowriter" ball point. National Geographic ad page: $3.

Sheaffer tried to keep fountain pen sales up in the 1950s by offering new models. The TM stood for "Thin Model" and was a slimmer, sleeker pen than previous models. Sheaffer was still using the white dot symbol, calling it "the white dot of distinction." National Geographic ad page from May 1952: $2.

"Skrip", which Sheaffer advertised as the "successor to ink," was developed by the company in 1922. The company avoided using the word "ink" in its advertisements for the product. An ad from 1929 states:

If you believe that all writing fluids are alike, you don't know Skrip. Think – Skrip cannot clog your pen! Because of its guarded formula, Skrip remains forever fluid in pens, yet, dries quicker on paper. Skrip-filled pens write instantly and without stutter or blot. A joy to use! In a Sheaffer's Lifetime Pen, peer of writing instruments, Skrip forms the finest alliance of all."

In the early 1930s, Sheaffer again proved an innovative leader in the pen industry with the introduction of its bullet shaped pens. These stream-lined models were known as "a balance-to-fit-the hand" pen. Sheaffer cornered the mid-price market from the late 1920s to the early 1940s. Because of the popularity of their design innovations, Sheaffer sold a great volume of pens during the Golden Years of the fountain pen. Because of their numbers, not their quality, Sheaffer pens are not considered nearly as desirable today as are the products of Parker, Waterman, Wahl-Eversharp, and Conklin.

THE SMALLER PENMAKER

Although the big three companies held the lion's share of the market, smaller pen companies abounded in the first half of the twentieth century. Many of these companies only lasted a few years or were bought out by one of the larger companies. One of the most interesting of these smaller, lesser-known companies is the Joseph Lipic Pen Company.

Founded by George L. Berg in 1853, the firm was originally called the Berg Company and headquartered in a one-room shop at 310 Olive Street, on the St. Louis Riverfront. In this shop, Mr. Berg made exceptionally fine pens for wooden and pearl inlaid penholders before the invention of the fountain pen.

Penmanship was a major accomplishment in this period, and individuals used different sized and pointed pens to achieve their particular writing style. Fine penmanship was a requisite for bookkeepers, clerks, shippers, and all who corresponded, did personal advertising, mailed bills or receipts; in fact, for most whom were in any way involved with commerce.

Mr. Berg devised a process for making superior gold nibs that were responsive to the writer's style. He sold from door to door, concentrating mainly on law offices, insurance companies, and realtors. In time, however, doctors, engineers, draftsmen, and merchants became exclusive users of his products.

The St. Louis Agricultural and Mechanical Exhibition at Fairground Park, which began on October 14, 1874, gave Berg an opportunity to exhibit his products to the general public on a large scale. For the excellence of these writing instruments he received a citation from Exhibition officials, signed in ink with his own points.

In order to produce such a gold nib it was necessary to melt a quantity of 14 karat gold and then roll it almost to the thinness of paper. This metal was then tempered, die-cut, and formed to the proper shape. This process gave the pen the desired flexibility necessary to accommodate the highly developed writing styles of the time, usually Spencerian, which shaded and gave character to signatures, figures, or words. This type of writing is still found on deeds, parchments, and diplomas.

After the gold nib was formed, small grains of a very hard ore called iridium, imported from Tasmania, were soldered to the tip. This grain, much smaller than the head of a pin, was hand-ground and polished by a slow and painstaking process. The grain was then split on a hair-thin wheel to allow the ink to be carried to the paper. Sometimes it would shatter into dust, adding frustration to this minute process.

The point of the pen, whether it be gold, silver, or steel, is actually never written on. Gold was principally used to give the writer softness and flexibility. Gold, if strained or put out of shape, almost immediately comes back to its original shape. The tiny ball of iridium is the only part of the pen point that actually touches the writing surface. Iridium is almost as hard as a diamond and will easily wear for 50 years or more if not damaged or injured.

Nib-holders were usually made of wood, but individuals demanded some fashioned in hand carved gold filigree design with accents and decorations of sterling silver and mother-of-pearl. The usual wooden lead pencil was also abandoned by some for a semi-automatic pencil of gold, silver, or pearl. Three or four inches long, these pencils were often carried by women on a chain around their neck or by men on a watch chain. The Berg Company made all of these variations.

Invention of a pen by L.E. Waterman that could be filled with an eye dropper and would write as long as a week without refilling brought about a great change in pen design and manufacture.

Joseph Lipic, Sr., then a baker by trade and the son-in-law of Mr. Berg, joined him in this

enterprise in 1904. He soon displayed an instinctive talent for this trade: mechanical ingenuity, inventive powers, and sales ability. From that year expansion was constant. The firm hired craftsman as demand steadily increased and word of these superior instruments spread to other cities. Salesmen extended their territories, and shipping increased rapidly.

Joseph Lipic eventually took over as head of the company. In 1910, he patented one of the finest self-filling fountain pens and it was put into manufacture. This was known as Lipic's "Radium Point Pen," and the improved method of filling is still the one in general use by all firms today. The Radium Point was sold to druggists, jewelers, and stationers within a 100-mile radius of St. Louis, and the trade name became the Joseph Lipic Pen Company. Expansion was in response to the demand of hundreds of stores in the United States and Mexico. Lipic's became known as "The Pen House of St. Louis."

The firm enlarged its range of services far beyond the manufacture of pens and pencils. Damaged gold nibs were repointed, and such outstanding firms as the W.A. Sheaffer Pen

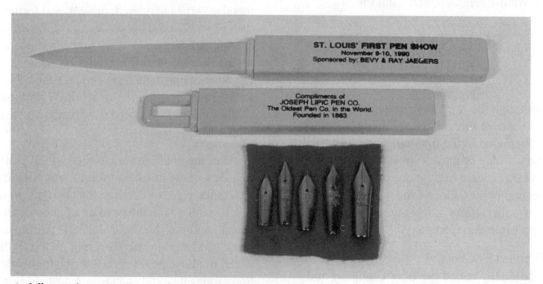

A full set of antique Lipic nibs in solid gold as made by the Lipic Company since 1904. Joseph Berg created the prototypes, amongst the very first gold nibs, in 1863. Each is worth a small amount as gold, but have more value as history: $5-$25 each (courtesy of Leonard Lipic). The pullout letter opener was created for the first St. Louis pen and inkwells show hosted by the authors in 1990: $30.

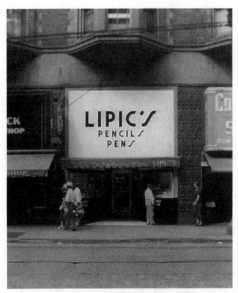

One of Lipic's downtown St. Louis shops, circa 1940.

Company engaged Lipic's services for repointing.

The firm moved four times to larger quarters. In 1922, Mr. Lipic located at 811 Locust Street and established, with his sons Joseph Jr., Sylvester, Walter, Emil, Leonard, and his two daughters, Gertrude (Mrs. Russell M. Wheeler), and Marie (Mrs. Michael V. Pheelan), the largest and only exclusive pen and pencil store in the world at that time. In fact, according to information given at the time by the Sheaffer and Parker families, it was also the first privately owned pen store in the world.

This store was, and is, wholly devoted to the selling and servicing of all makes of fine writing instruments, providing the wholesaler, retailer, and consumer with the largest display of domestic and foreign writing instruments ever seen in one location. The finest pens and pencils of the world can be found here, and special pens have been designed for court reporters, stenographers, and musicians.

In 1936, Lipic's moved again to larger quarters at 813 Locust Street.

During World War II, shortage of materials decreased the supply, but Lipic's allotment was one of the largest in the country, based on previous volume. On some days long lines of customers blocked the sidewalks waiting their turn to purchase.

Joseph Lipic Pen Company has received several awards for their fine artwork in reproducing advertising copy on the various items they manufacture. Due to their fine quality and workmanship, they have been privileged to manufacture pens for former President Johnson, President Nixon, Vice President Agnew, Pope Paul VI, and numerous religious and governmental dignitaries throughout the world. These pens carry a reproduction of the individual's signature and the seal of the office that they hold.

Lipic Pen Company remains in business at 2200 Gravois Avenue in St. Louis. Today they make all types of ballpoint pens and desk items for incentive companies who put their logo on these items.

G51-15 **Pocket Pal Pencil.** By Lipic! Dainty gift for the ladies in the family! Gay tassel adorns the end of each colorful pencil, makes it easy to find in handbag or pocket. Has handy extra lead chamber and eraser. Beautifully gift boxed. Each _ _ _ _ _ _ _ _ _ _ _ **$1.00**
Stationery—Main Floor

The "Pocket Pal" pencil was one of the many products made by the Lipic Company.

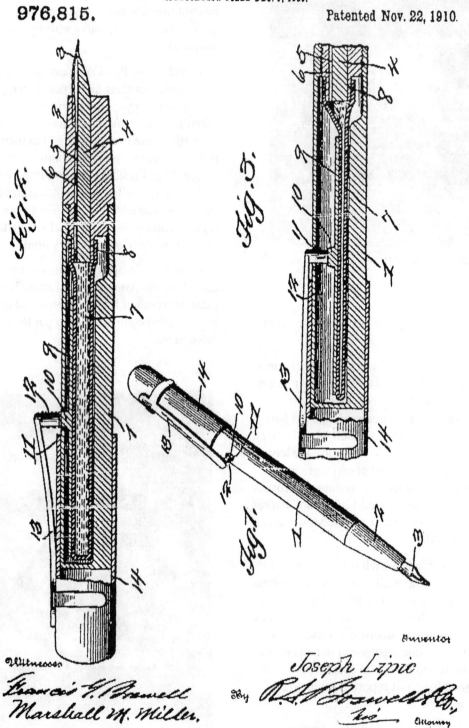

An original patent drawing for the pull lever filler which was granted in 1910. Joseph Lipic Pen Company was never given credit for this amazingly useful invention, which became the standard and state of the art in 1915. Lipic made inkwells and desk pieces from 1890 to today.

A Lipic sales representative mans the booth at a tradeshow in Cleveland, Ohio. On the left is a display of Boy Scouts pencils. Lipic made many of the bullet-type advertising pencils that were popular in the 1930s-1950s.

Known as the "Pen Corner of St. Louis," Lipic's store on the corner of 8th and Olive streets was located directly across the street from the Post Office.

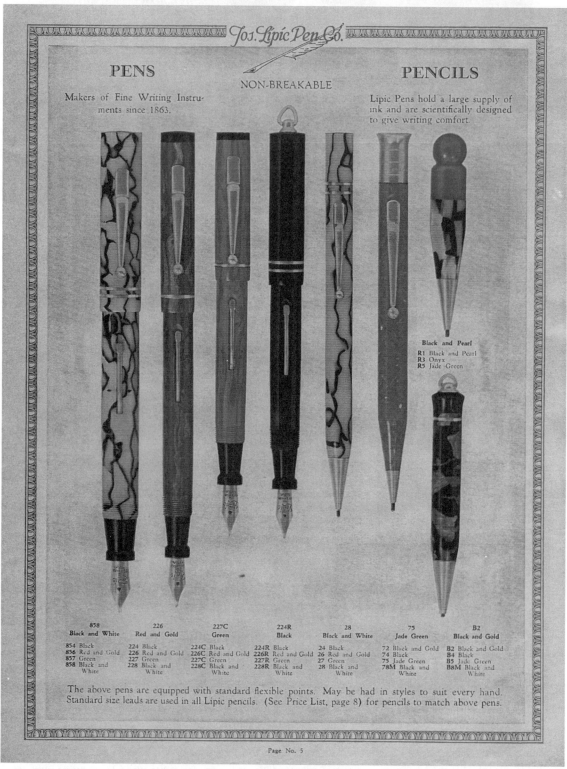

A catalog page, circa 1925, featuring pens and pencils available from the Joseph Lipic Pen Compnay.

Sheaffer "balance" pens in inkwell. This rare set is of the blood-veined marble 1930's: $65 set.

These excellent examples of woodcarving hail from Germany's Black Forest area. Tourism became an industry in the middle years of the 1800's. When oceanic travel became feasible upon the invention of the steamer, souvenirs followed just behind the influx of tourists.
(Left) Bear with open mouth, acorn cap on pressed glass well insert. 3 inches by 5 inches: $250.
(Right) Closed-mouth bear on smaller pedestal. 3 inches by 3-7/8 inches: $100 for stand missing cap.

Another view of the inkstand showing the bear with open mouth Extremely fine detailing: $250 and up.

The manufacturers of the Bengal tiger inkwell made at least four and perhaps as many as six sizes and styles of inkstands by using more or less of the mold. This one, which includes shoulders and paws on crossed forearms, is somewhat ungainly and awkward. It's size alone would keep it off any but a baronial desk. It is 5-1/2 inches tall by 5-1/2 inches deep and 4-3/4 inches wide. One has been found with a Merider Con label. Prices range from $300-$400 for head alone, to $450 for head and neck, to $150-$250 for head, shoulders and paws, depending on condition.

Black ram's head inkwell made of cast iron. The head is hinged and lifts to reveal the inset well. Unusual to find with both horns still intact. Late 1800's: $95.

Bronze peacock or long-tailed birds, double stand, of a type popular in France. Tiffany made a design so similar there is some questions about the maker. The matching letter holder hints that there were more pieces in the set. Late 1800's: $750-$800.

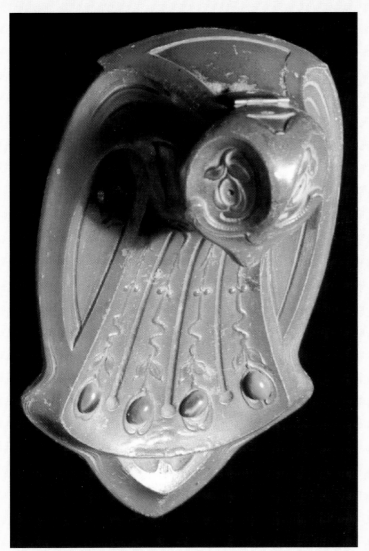

Early example of unusual style featuring a mid-1800s cannon with a large wicker basket and powder flashes. The basket contains a small, snap-lidded travel well with a blown glass insert: $480.

Extremely stylized fan-tailed owl with semi-precious stone inserts. The head lifts to expose a glass insert. Bronze, 1900-1920: $450.

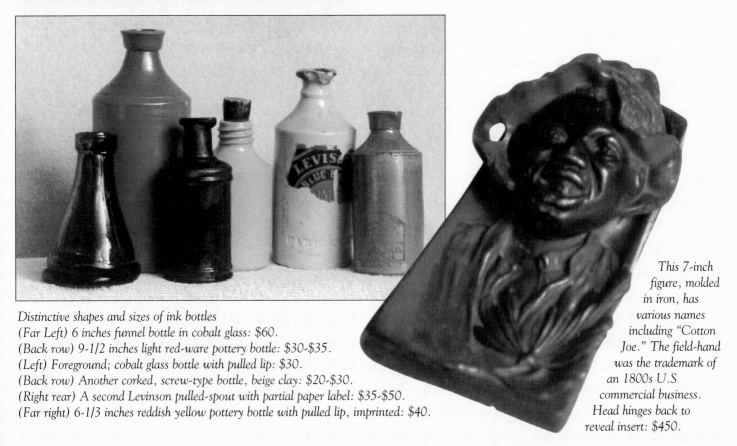

Distinctive shapes and sizes of ink bottles
(Far Left) 6 inches funnel bottle in cobalt glass: $60.
(Back row) 9-1/2 inches light red-ware pottery bottle: $30-$35.
(Left) Foreground; cobalt glass bottle with pulled lip: $30.
(Back row) Another corked, screw-type bottle, beige clay: $20-$30.
(Right rear) A second Levinson pulled-spout with partial paper label: $35-$50.
(Far right) 6-1/3 inches reddish yellow pottery bottle with pulled lip, imprinted: $40.

This 7-inch figure, molded in iron, has various names including "Cotton Joe." The field-hand was the trademark of an 1800s U.S commercial business. Head hinges back to reveal insert: $450.

Three clear glass wells
(Left) Drape Rollproof: $11.
(Middle) Crystal lidded apple, 2-7/8 inches: $45.
(Right) Blown mold Sanford's: $7.50

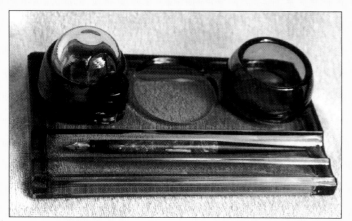

The all-purpose desk unit in shamrock green glass. The 'bubble' ink container on the left was set in a squared catch basin. Center may be designed for extra nibs and paper clips. Bowl-type receptacle on right may have held a damp sponge to clean nibs and fingers. These units rarely survive in fine condition and with attachments. 7-1/2 inches by 10 inches: $115 -$130.

(Left) Early blown molded cobalt well with pour lip, 4 inches tall. Marked SS STAFFORD'S INK USA: $50.
(Right) Early 18th Century hand blown ink, deep cobalt, 4 inches tall. Rolled lip: $75.

Loetz Art Nouveau blue and purple shaded 'Brocade' glass with flowing haired beauty on cap: $450-$500.

Very old, and probably one of a kind, this pinkish bronze 6 inch diameter piece is marked "real bronze" on base. The lid features a mythological human warrior battling a dragon wearing a sword, high cap, and barefoot. He holds a very ancient style of shield. Celtic designs complete the lid design which hinge-backs to a white insert: $800-1000.

Side detailing shows three sailing ships of different types in high relief. Curling waves and storm clouds surround the ships. Inkwells of this type are often story-telling wells whose detailing is of ancient legends and heroes. At auction this unique piece might exceed $1000.

Rex, King of Carnival, may be the inspiration for this baroque footed double-inkstand. The crowned figure backs a lidded compartment designed to hold nibs and tools. In light polished brass, this fine 1800's piece measures 15-1/2 inches by 4-1/2 inches and contains double hinge-back lids concealing white glass well inserts: $550.

Bronze well made by Tiffany is an octagonal shape. Large well measures 8 inches by 8 inches. Bookmark pattern. The lift-back lid conceals a single glass insert. $450.

An enormous inkstand designed only for the desk of an executive or a writer. The crystal inkwells hold a half-pint of ink! This light-bronze piece is 8-1/2 inches by 12 inches. Made in 1890-1900. Its aura is of sheer elegance. Truly unique! $2500-$3000.

The allure of the Middle East is evident in this brass and enamel piece with its 6-1/2 inch diameter reverse-plate and finial on top of the hinge-back lid. Lid lifts to reveal a metal insert: $155-$200.

Art Nouveau was the inspiration for this lovely set with its gleaming fluid lines and lustrous geometric accents, 12 inches by 4-1/2 inches. Light bronze, it is of American make and reputed by its former owner to be a Tiffany piece given to a friend, thus remaining uncatalogued and unreproduced. Lovely and unique, its floriform lines and swirled petalling are indeed a favorite theme of Louis Comfort Tiffany: $1500-$2000.

Artistically, the English were supreme in Victorian brass-work of this type. The handled tray seems designed for royalty and perhaps it was. Double glass wells are concealed by hinge-back finish of baroque styling: $1100.

A mystery well of worked iron, 3-1/2 inches deep by 3-1/4 inches wide. The mystery consists of the large aperture in front of the tray. There is no hint as to its purpose. Black washed iron: $50.

Imported English pewter wells feature unusual styling and small size. The Mary Poppins like charwoman is traditional. 3-1/4 inches hinge-back on left conceals white glass insert: $205. Dove on right is probably originally an insert from a larger unit. Also a hinge-back with white porcelain insert. Note black rim at base: $80.

Massive yet graceful, a domed hinge-back lid caps this lordly inkwell. Pomegranate-like floral designs embellish the piece. Inkwell $120, calendar frame $40, rocker blotter $70.

These rotary ball wells were made in six or seven colors of glass and various types of plastics. Color combinations include white, black and tan, black and red, and all black. Set in concave square holders, these balls swivel to any position: $65-$110.

These shell inkstands often carried a painted or glued-on advertising message for a seaside resort.
(Left) Shell cut to appear fish-like, 5 inches long: $50 (ink-well set into top of head.)
(Right) A concretion-style, glass well covered in sea pebbles and shell bits. A double shell at rear holds a pen steady. Metal screw-off cap: $95-$100.

Neo-classical styling and high relief make this double stand and clock an unusual 1920's piece; note porcelain inserts: $130.

Elegant curvilinear desk piece including pen-catcher, crystal well, and attached utility box with hinge-back lid 14 inches by 8 inches: $105.

Double moose with calf design in light bronze with Eversharp pen-catcher: $225.

An elegant transitional piece from the period when inkwell molds were re-tooled to include a generic pen-catcher, 8 inches by 13 inches, solid brass: $550.

Single figural model, unknown maker with enameled bronze dog: $50-$60 each.

Eversharp became the only company name of Wahl-Eversharp in the mid 1930's. This "Greek key" set is named for the design of the bands on the caps. The small gold dot near the top contained a double check mark, which was the company's guarantee of perfect workmanship. If found with a tiny hole drilled into this spot, it means Eversharp repaired the pen and the original guarantee is void. Both pen and pencil should have the seal to be considered a set. In box: $250.

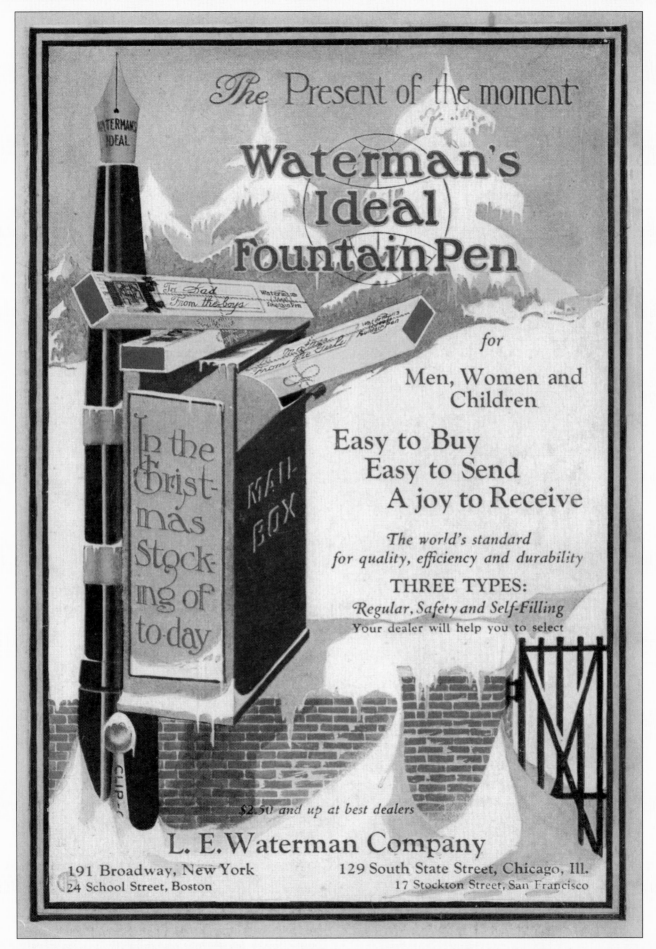

*Back cover Christmas ad for Waterman's pens. Pens located in perfect condition and in their Holiday boxes may bring a 10 %
higher price. Pen shown is a smooth hard black rubber eyedropper filler. Pen $40 to $200. Scribner's ad page from December
1920, $3.50.*

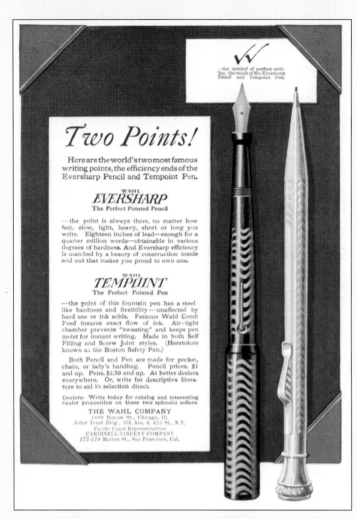

In color, this ad introduced the double check mark as the Eversharp guarantee. The pencil design is pre-1900, althouh the ad is from 1918. Pen valued at $45 and up, pencil in sterling silver $75, in silver-plate $50. Harper's ad page, $3.

Esterbrook ad page showing several of the points available for their pens. Esterbrook was a leading maker of steel pens in the nineteenth century, but got into the fountain pen market a bit late in the game. Esterbrook made a dependable, inexpensive pen that was widely used in the waning days of the fountain pen. National Geographic ad page from September 1950: $2.

The Pen made for the ink —the Ink made for the pen

A PEN and a bottle of Ink become a big topic through the magic of science. For physicists, chemists and engineers now return from their 11-year quest into the strange world of physical and chemical phenomena bearing the prize of their search.

Yes, they sought and they found a Pen and an Ink "made for each other" —a pen that starts in a split-second—a "high velocity" Ink that dries ON PAPER as you write—a combination that writes with pencil-like ease.

The only Pen that will handle this speed-drying Ink, yet a pen that will handle ANY writing ink to perfection, if thoroughly cleansed before filling with a new variety.

Still all this search came near to failure when the scientists discovered that this Ink lost its speed-drying magic when exposed to air. Yet it must be used in the open.

Then a Nobel Prize winner propounded a theory that surmounted this last obstacle. And Parker chemists successfully applied it by making a screen of inactive molecules to form on the ink *and shield its speed-drying properties from air attacks!* Thus air and climate do not affect it.

Victory at last—the Parker "51" Pen and "51" Ink. Try them today at any nearby pen counter, and see them perform their miracles for *you*.

COPR. 1942, THE PARKER PEN CO., JANESVILLE, WIS.

Parker "51"

INDIA BLACK · CORDOVAN BROWN · DOVE GRAY · BLUE CEDAR

Dries as you write

YEARS AHEAD OF ITS TIME...TWELVE-FIFTY AND FIFTEEN DOLLARS

◆ GUARANTEED BY LIFE CONTRACT—Parker's Blue Diamond on the pen is our Contract unconditionally Guaranteeing service for the owner's Life, without cost other than 35¢ charge for postage, insurance and handling, if pen is not intentionally damaged and is returned complete.

1942 ad for the revolutionary Parker "51." The pen featured a "hooded" nib and was designed to be used with Parker's quick-drying "51" ink. New Yorker ad from April 1942: $3.50.

This group of pens represents the Joseph Lipic Company's variety of products in the 1920's and '30's. Lipic made blank barrels and caps for most of the major "big 4" pen-makers so similarities of style are often noted between their products and a Lipic. Lipic however, never put their name on the pocket clips, so that they are hard to differentiate. Lipic also made such excellent nibs that customers often brought in their pens to have a Lipic nib installed. Values for a mint hard black rubber Lipic pen would be $40-$50 for #2 & #4, while #1 & #3 would be $25-$35 and #5 would bring $45 or more if mint. (Courtesy Leonard Lipic)

Lipic Centennial in 1963 marked the 100th year of pen making for the St. Louis company: $75 and up.

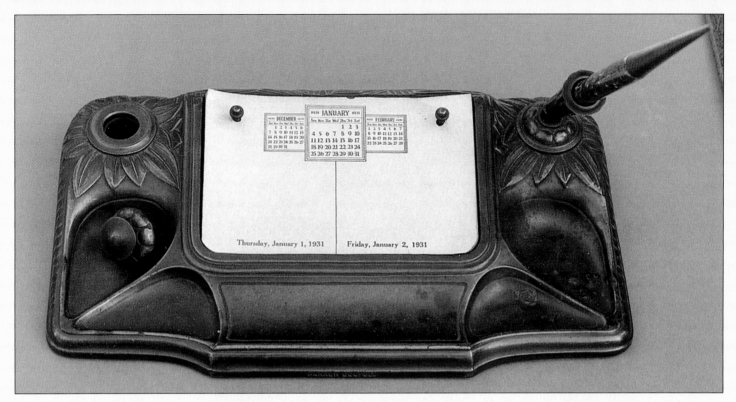

Bronze inkstand by Parker Pen Co. features bronze over wood in a styled Deco motif. Rare to find one with calendar and ink stopper: $450.

Green glass desk piece produced by Sheaffer for their 1930's pens: $65 each.

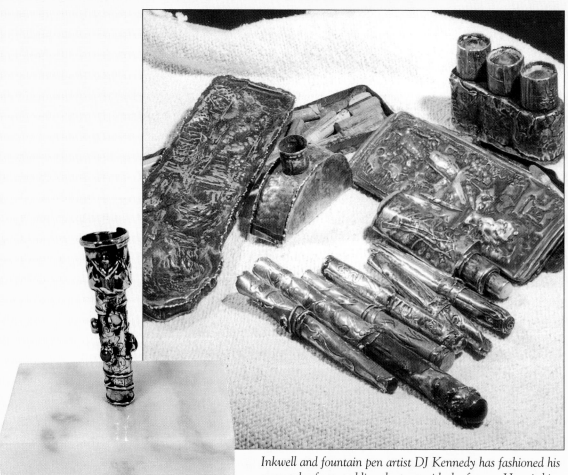

Pen-catcher for the D.J. Kennedy clip pen.
Its swirl-embellished surface is studded with
cabochon gems and set in onyx.

Inkwell and fountain pen artist DJ Kennedy has fashioned his
own styles from melding the past with the future. Here is his
'art kit' in solid silver with accents of other metals.

With a simple addition of silver cap to inkwell, and sheath to pen, Kennedy creates pieces of lasting beauty and artistic value.

114

Stunning bronze and art glass 16 inches by 7 inches. Art Deco lamps graced library tables and side tables in offices accompanied by a bronze tray into which visitors placed their calling cards: $325 and up.

French 19th century light bronze three-piece set. This set accompanied a university professor to this country in 1893 and was still in the possession of his son (also a university professor), when sold in 1985. The epitome of the Art Nouveau naturalistic era, the grape and vine motif is charming, and the lovebirds on the inkwell are exquisite. The most unusually designed inkwell conceals two cobalt blue glass inserts. Set $3500-$5000 at auction. Inkwell $2000, rocker blotter $400, letter rack $750.

Light pine wood glass lid, container glass lidded well, rocker blotter, quill knife and steel point dip-pen on lift out tray: $95.

The coveted blue glass of 1920's vintage and extreme Deco styling makes this set charmingly original and different! Glass and chrome set $225. Individual pieces calendar and base $60, pen-catcher $50 and rocker blotter $75-$80.

Stylized "fish" paperweight. Fish is a touch-lift. In bronze, this may be a fraternal symbol 7 inches by 3-1/2 inches: $115.

A triply attractive weight from a pharmaceutical manufacturer. A very collectible item: $65-80.

These less expensive paperweights are often given a paper label on their base or affixed to their sides. This one is desirable as an example of embedded air-bubbles: $45.

Group of three "millefiore" (million flowers) advertising paperweights. Values range from $25-$60 each.

Glass weight features a young Shirley Temple.
Probably early 1940's souvenir: $50.

Dome weights from a National Shrine, $30, and an aquarium in Florida, $40 (objects actually embedded in the glass itself.)

Group of three dome paperweights with advertising messages.
(Left) "Ft. Worth" cowboy 1930's: $30.
(Rear) Memento of Worlds Fair 1904 "The Communications Building, St. Louis, MO:" $65.
(Right) "Rocky Mt. National Park" about 1930: $25-30.

118

Three sizes of what are called 'cathedral' ink bottles in cobalt blue glass with raised cathedral-window designs largest $65 - $80. Medium size $70 (hardest to find), smaller $45 - 50 with intact label. Low-rider bottle for desk $40 (compliments of John Hinkel from his collection).

A quartet of extremely unusual ink containers. Ink often came in a dry, powdered form, or in small pellets to be re-mixed with water.
(Left) Box with stain $20
(Middle) Palmer's ink $40.
(Right) Box with stain $20 right
(Right Front) Box with no stain, small but perfect $35 - 55 with contents. (Compliments of John Hinkel)

A Carter Ink master bottle in cobalt with slightly torn label $20 up. (J. Hinkel)

Cobalt inks a century apart.
(Left) Funnel well cast in sand: $45.
(Right) Super Quink in art deco diamond shape bottle.

1930's inkbottles with original boxes add much to the collectibility of inks.
These include a diamond shaped Quink box: $12-$25 each.

Whole labels or unusual labels, as in these examples, boost prices to $10-$12 each. The older bottles on the center and right have cork tops, while the more recent bottle on the left has a screw on cap.

Modern Sanford's Pen it miniature bottles are easily collected and present themselves in many vibrant colors: $5 each.

Common bottles or damaged labels or caps lessen the value of inks: $2-$3 each.

Sanford's special "Penit" kept users from mistaking it for laundry bluing which came in identical bottles and was royal blue as well. Note unusual pour spout: $30 each with box; $20 each without. These old inks can be used in modern pens, especially if they are unopened. Inks like this with only a pint remaining should be strained through a piece of cotton rag into another bottle before using in a pen or restored antiques.

Carter's ink Master with a nice clean box, some ink and an unusual pouring spout makes a charming picture and may be used after straining: $45 each.

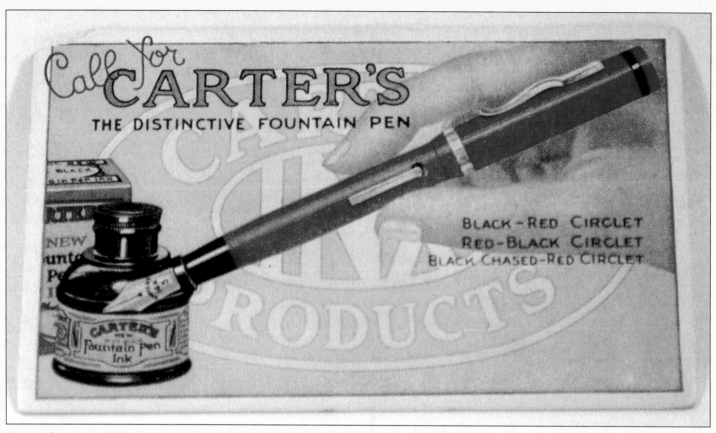

Carter advertising ink blotter was a popular give-away to customers: $20 each.

Tape measures hide within decorative objects and feature 20" to 36" fabric tapes with pullout attachments concealed inside.
(Left) Rocking horse with pullout: $45.
(Middle) 1920's Swiss peasant girl with 36" pullout, 3-1/2 inches high: $50-60.
(Right) Alloy bronze-finished horse with pullout: $25-35.

A 1940's pencil sharpener. This one brings in a higher value since it features Mickey Mouse in hard plastic full form: $120 and up.

Unusual wall-mounted chalkware holder. These were mounted in shops and home kitchens. Some are string-holders others have fabric measuring tapes inside. 6 inches tall. $45-50.

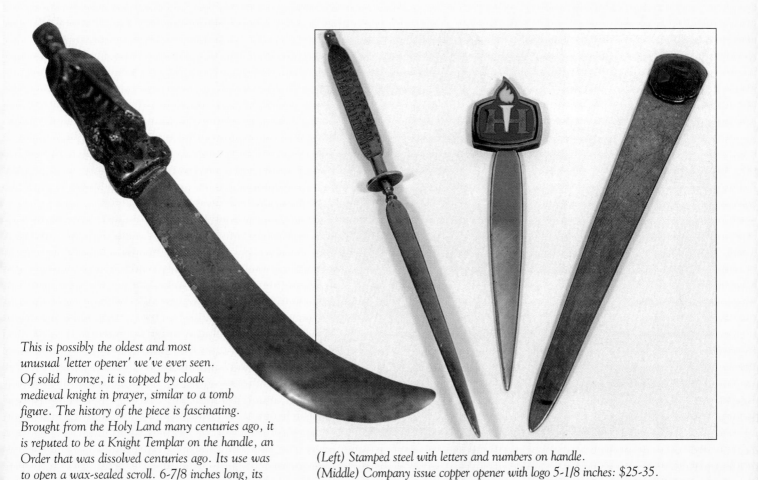

This is possibly the oldest and most unusual 'letter opener' we've ever seen. Of solid bronze, it is topped by cloak medieval knight in prayer, similar to a tomb figure. The history of the piece is fascinating. Brought from the Holy Land many centuries ago, it is reputed to be a Knight Templar on the handle, an Order that was dissolved centuries ago. Its use was to open a wax-sealed scroll. 6-7/8 inches long, its value up to or over $2500

(Left) Stamped steel with letters and numbers on handle.
(Middle) Company issue copper opener with logo 5-1/8 inches: $25-35.
(Bottom) Bronze opener with fused logo in coin-like shape at top 6-7/8 inches: $35-45.

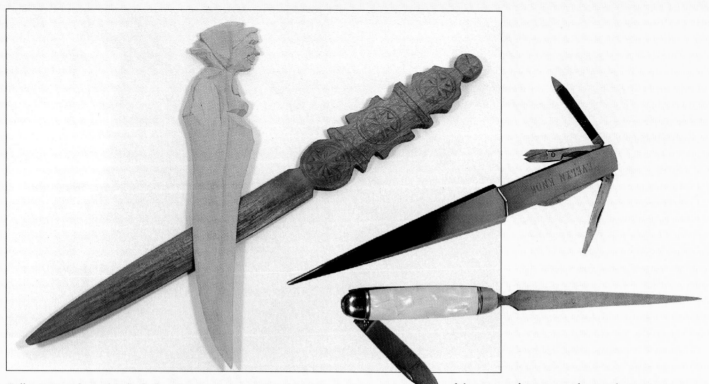

Folk art carved wood; whittled work openers are a delightful addition to any collection of openers.
(Left) Whimsical peasant woman from deep in the Ozarks made about 1950's 5-1/2 inches: $45.
(Right) Cookie press or quilt designs in wood similar to Amish styles. 6 inches: $40.

Most unusual openers with extra features.
(Top) Solingen steel opening to two knife blades, nail file and scissors. From Switzerland, 9 inches: $115.
(Bottom) An American entry with 'pocketknife' handle, one blade 9 inches: $110.

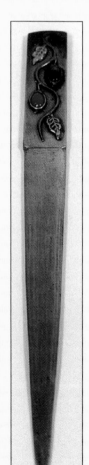

Inlaid bronze wire and cabochon 'gems' stud the handle of this one-piece opener, very simple idea 7-7/8 inches: $95.

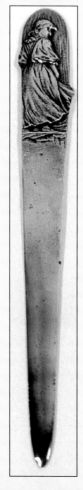

Unusual deeply formed peasant or gypsy woman's skirt being pulled, probably an invisible dog. 8-1/8 inches: $90.

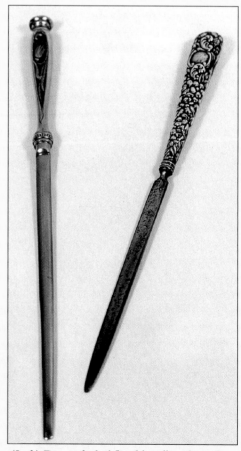

(Left) Deep relief of floral handle, silver-plate on steel 6-1/2 inches: $75.
(Right) Brass and steel. The handle features a lowly Art Nouveau flower: $60.

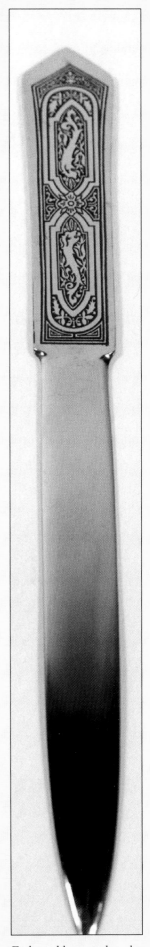

Trio of all brass letter-openers.
(Left) Gracefully curved 's' handle may be a special design: $45-60.
(Middle) Very Art Nouveau handle of floral and solar design. 8 inches $100.
(Right) Open-worked sculpture of large-hatted woman wearing a short bolero jacket. 7-1/2 inches: $90-100.

Embossed brass and steel with lovely dolphin motif on handle 7-3/4 inches: $105.

Fanciful and filled with symbols of heraldry, these worked brass with seal openers are still useful and decorative as paperweights if nothing else.
(Left) A royal lion with scepter in brass, standing on globe. 5-1/2 inches: $80.
(Right) Snake swallowing, another coming up the handle. 6-7/8 inches: $85-95.

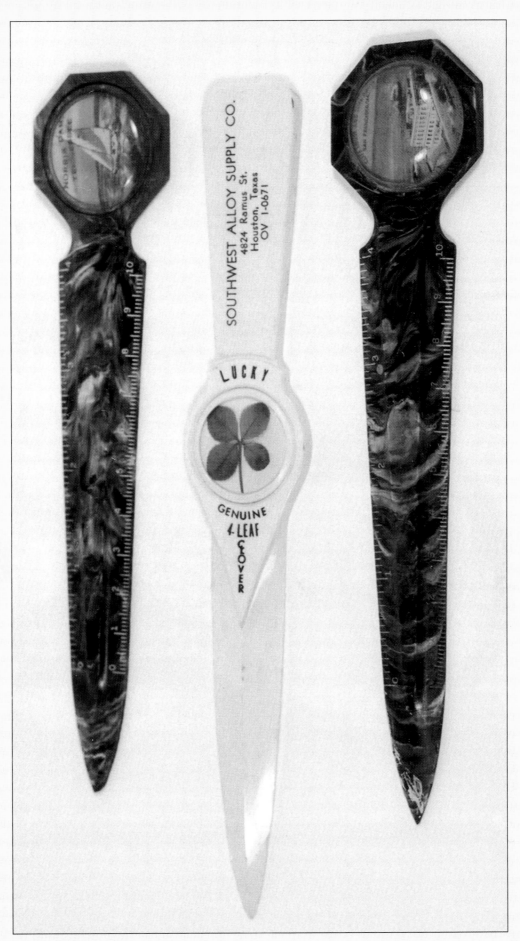

Trio of 1930's plastic tourist souvenirs
(Left) Bubble-style with sailboat: $25.
(Middle) Bubble with dried, pressed 4-leaf 'lucky' clover: $30.
(Right) Bubble handle with architectural feature: $20.

For offices before air-conditioning, these lovely and practical fans were welcomed by secretaries and provided name recognition at the same time. The most wanted are those with golf or railroad motifs: $25 and up.

Three all glass dip pens. They hold no ink, but have sharp knurled tips. Barrels may contain paper advertisements or pictures. Hand blown: $20-$40 each.

Unusual iron alloy inkwell with attached thermometer. These advertising items were actually useful and kept the name in front of the recipient: $95-$105.

CHAPTER 6

COLLECTING PENS

How many times have you looked at a fountain pen and wondered if it had value or was just a piece of junk? The few books on pens are expensive . . . should you buy them? If you decide to sell this item, should you clean it or repair it? What constitutes a desirable item, a pen collector's dream?

Many dealers and collectors avoid fountain pens entirely, as there are too many questions involved and too little general knowledge available. Although we may have used a fountain pen in grade school, the ballpoint is all powerful today. Old fountain pens are often considered too messy to bother with in many shops and malls.

A collector's treasure-trove of fountain pens. The display box is as collectible as the pens: $20-$100 depending on maker and age. All pens are from larger pen manufacturers and range from $25-100 each.

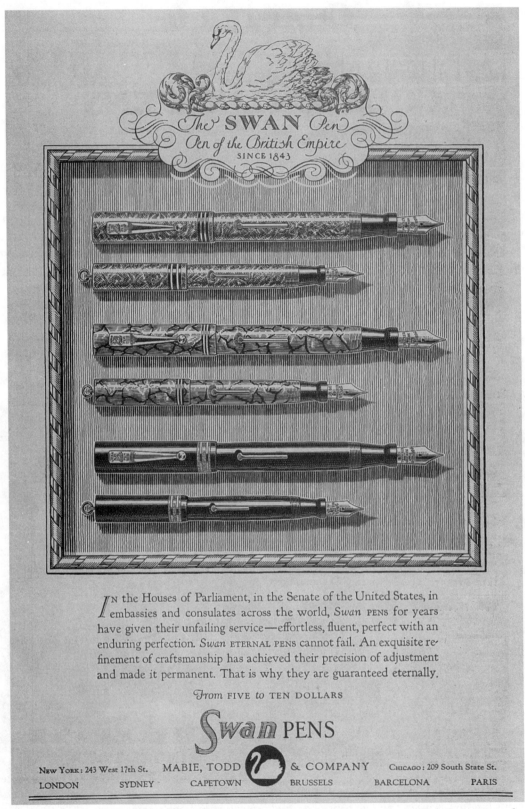

Swan pens, manufactured in England by the Mabie Todd Company, provided elegance in the 1920s and 1930s. 1929 National Geographic *ad page: $2.*

Ink-maker Carter started producing fountain pens in the late 1920s. This venture did not last more than a few years and proved unprofitable for the company. In those few years, however, they did produce some attractive pens and accessories. Mostly made of a pearlized plastic, this material usually yellowed with age. Some of the larger models appeared in colors like light blue and are very scarce today. 1930 Literary Digest ad page: $2.

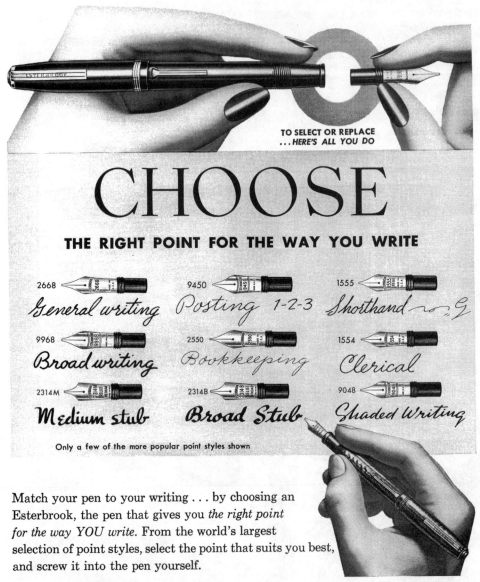

Match your pen to your writing . . . by choosing an Esterbrook, the pen that gives you *the right point for the way YOU write*. From the world's largest selection of point styles, select the point that suits you best, and screw it into the pen yourself.

And remember, in case of damage, your Esterbrook point is *instantly* renewable, at any pen counter.

POCKET SET—Esterbrook Pen and matching Push-Pencil. Pencil holds two feet of lead. Writes for months without reloading. Standard or thin lead models. "Push the top to feed the lead."

FOUNTAIN PEN
ESTERBROOK—AMERICA'S PEN NAME SINCE 1858

COPYRIGHT 1952—THE ESTERBROOK PEN COMPANY

Mention the National Geographic—It identifies you

Esterbrook was a leading manufacturer of pen points, and stressed this strength in their advertising. This 1952 ad shows some of the pen points available, and the writing styles one could achieve with these points. National Geographic *ad from 1952: $1.*

Group of inexpensive pens. The pen second from left was made by Wearever.

Most dealers will never encounter the exquisite silver or gold-laced sheathed pens we've all heard about. It is much more likely that you will be asked to buy or to bid on a handful of miscellaneous and colorful pens of the 1930 to 1950 era. Most of these pens will have minimal values, but there may well be one pen in this cigar box or group which can net you a tidy profit.

I have personally seen such colorful but common pens as Esterbrook and Wearever being offered at prices from well under fifty dollars to almost a hundred, depending on the mall. Sometimes these will be the only brands visible, even in a very large establishment with many dealers. When questioned, mall owners and individual dealers report that they avoid pens like the plague, as they know nothing of their condition and value.

Esterbrook, a company that began in the mid-1800s, was primarily known as a maker of dip pens and steel points. They did not produce fountain pens in great numbers until the 1940s and 1950s, when fountain pen popularity was waning. However, Esterbrook pens sold in great numbers, as every schoolchild was encouraged to buy one when learning cursive writing in the higher grades of school. They took rough handling. Nibs could be exchanged for a more suitable flexibility, and they seemed to last forever. Esterbrooks, along with the less desirable

Wearever, are the most often encountered pens in antique shops today.

Neither Esterbrook nor Wearever pens had gold nibs, and this seems to make them less desirable. However, if you are just looking for a piece of nostalgia, Esterbrook models are usually easily repaired and may be used with liquid ink. Valuation is reasonable at $10 to $15; $20 if the pen is an unusual pastel color or if there is a pencil to match.

Wearever pens were less well-made, and are almost valueless to a collector. They are harder to repair and generally considered not worth the effort.

With the lever-filling pen, in all cases, do not attempt to lift the lever to see "if the pen works" as it may completely ruin the pen and render it unrepairable.

GOLD NIBS

During the frantic "gold surge" of a few years ago, many persons ignorant of the value of an intact antique pen, ripped off the gold nib and rushed to the jeweler to turn it in for cash. In this way, thousands of vintage writing instruments were vandalized, and a great many were completely destroyed.

Trio of pen nibs. On the left is a Sheaffer example of the "hooded" type which was made popular by the Parker 51. In the center is an Esterbrook steel nib, and on the right is a Parker.

Most nibs on fountain pens of the big pen makers were made of gold. Gold was more malleable than steel, making for a more flexible point. Because gold is so soft, the very hard metal iridium was added at the very tip to prevent the point from wearing down. Many pen companies may have added beautiful scrolling designs to their nibs, or labeled them with the company name.

Even if you locate a pen that has no nib at all, or has a good gold nib with a broken barrel or cap, you should not assume that the item has no value. First, the nib alone may be just the part that you need to restore your vintage pen. Secondly, many collectors will buy a fine pen that has all its parts except the nib. Serious pen collectors trade parts back and forth to restore their collections to their original splendor.

I have had many calls from dealers or sellers who assume that just the fact that a pen has a gold nib makes it valuable. Sorry to say, that tiny amount of gold is negligible; not worth pulling off the pen to melt down. Keep all pieces of any broken pen together, as you may want all the parts you can use later.

MAKERS' MARKS

A magnifying glass, preferably with a light, is the best help in identifying old fountain pens. Their names are usually on the gold nib, as well as somewhere on the barrel's side. Large pen companies tended to mark their products clearly and almost all of these incised names and designs are still readable under magnification.

A 1990s renaissance of the Parker Duofold. Parker's distinctive arrow logo is still prominent on the clips. Postcard announcement from the Seattle Pen Company 1992: $4.

Conklin pens are easily identified by the distinctive crescent filler Pressing down the crescent emptied the rubber bladder, which on release would fill with ink. Harper's Magazine *ad page from 1918: $2.*

If a maker's trademark appears on the pen barrel and another is on the nib, this may be a sign that the pen has been fitted with a pirated nib just so that is will look good. In some cases, the pirated nib may be much more valuable than the pen and barrel.

Parker began using the famous arrow design on its clips in the 1930s. The arrow had been used in print advertising and was a familiar logo to many. Waterman pens were usually marked with that company's globe logo, signifying their world wide sales. Sheaffer not only individually numbered its Lifetime pens, but also added a white dot above the clip making the pen instantly recognizable.

The Conklin Pen Company, whose pens were adorned with a golden crescent filler toward the end of the barrel, used a system of name and numbers to identify their products. If the golden crescent is sunken in, it is merely because the hardened ink sac has collapsed inward. The number will still appear in the black barrel toward the back end of the pen. Wahl-Eversharp used a double check emblem, which resembled the W of their name, on their higher end pens. Some of these were on the barrel sideways rather than lengthwise, and the pen must be carefully examined under a good light to determine if this is the case. They also made a tiny pen, not much longer than a wooden match, which is quite collectible, as are all miniature pens.

DESK PENS

Desk sets for fountain pens became popular in the 1920s. Similar sets had existed for dip pens so they were not exactly a new innovation. These sets consisted of a base with a socket attached to hold the pen. All of the major pen makers made desk-type pens which were sometimes designed to either leave on the businessman's desk, or to pocket and take along to a meeting. Desk pens were made with a tapering end that fit into the desk penholder. The larger pen companies made pens that could be converted to pocket models by unscrewing them

from the base and putting on a cap. Parker specialized in these convertible-pens during the 1920s, and a number of their famed Duofold pens were designed as convertibles. Parker desk sets were most likely to come in marbleized green. The discovery of a desk set in one of the rarer Duofold colors, such as lapis or yellow, is an uncommon event for any dealer or collector.

Many of these desk pens included a small black taper that could be screwed on at the back of the pen if it was to be kept in a desk holder for any length of time. Many of these did not survive, but if some are encountered in a cigar box, they should be washed and kept until the appropriate desk holder is found.

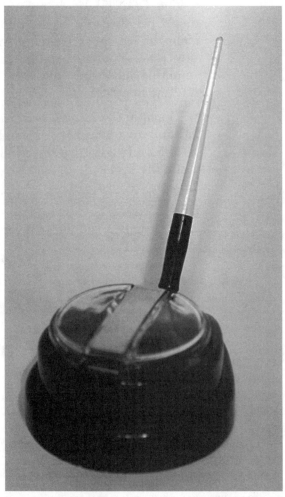

Late 1920s Bakelite-type desk well with steel and glass cover. Simple style was often found in office settings: $60.

Desk bases are, of course, collectible, and if marked by one of major makers, Parker, Waterman, Eversharp, or Conklin, will bring modest prices from another collector or form the nucleus of one's own collection.

Comb-back green onyx base with pen-catcher: $40.

New Fountain Pen Desk Set Holds Pencil, Too

Both Convertible for Pocket and Desk

Pen Guaranteed for Life

Here is the newest and loveliest gift of all—for blushing bride or clear-eyed graduate—for birthdays, young and old, or anniversary.

Parker Fountain Pens and Pencils—in breathtaking beauty of color—now come in combination sets for desk or pocket, for the first time.

And both pen and pencil—also for the first time—are *convertible* for instant pocket or Desk Set use by merely changing caps for tapered tip, or reverse.

When you get the desk base—either now or later—you get included, the graceful tapered ends you need for desk use. You also get the gold-trimmed pocket caps with clip for pocket use. Thus you get *double duty* from the pen that is Guaranteed for Lite.

Pen Guaranteed for Life

The famous Parker Pressureless Touch—Non-breakable barrels—17.4% greater ink capacity, size for size—Parker's Guarantee for Life—these important features, exclusive in Parker, settle all doubts as to choice.

Parker streamlined pens and pencils come in matched pairs—with or without Desk Bases. In mandarin yellow, jewel-like jade, lacquer red, jet-like black-and-gold, lapis lazuli blue... and in de luxe black-and-pearl, newest color of all.

Select your gift from the wide range at any fountain pen counter. Look for the imprint "Geo. S. Parker—DUOFOLD" on the pen barrel—your Guarantee for Life. Pens, $5 to $10. Pencils to match, $3.25 to $5. Bases, $4 and up.

THE PARKER PEN COMPANY, Janesville, Wis.

Something NEW

"Vest-Parker" Pens—Guaranteed for Life—and Pencils to Match

Midget Parker Duofolds—convertible for use in pocket or Desk Set. Cuddle comfortably in your hand when writing, snuggle unobtrusively in pocket like a latchkey. The pen $5, the pencil $2.50.

JUNE GIFTS—*Graduations—Birthdays—Weddings—Anniversaries*

Duofold Senior black-and-pearl convertible Pen and Pencil with polished onyx Base, $26. With Duofold Junior Pen and Pencil, $23.50.

Parker Duofold
$5 $7 $10
PEN GUARANTEED FOR LIFE

Parker Pressureless Touch

A stylish and attractive Parker Duofold convertible desk set from 1930. National Geographic ad page: $2.

A Walgreen Drug special desk piece and pen. Green pens and onyx were a Walgreen's hallmark: $12.

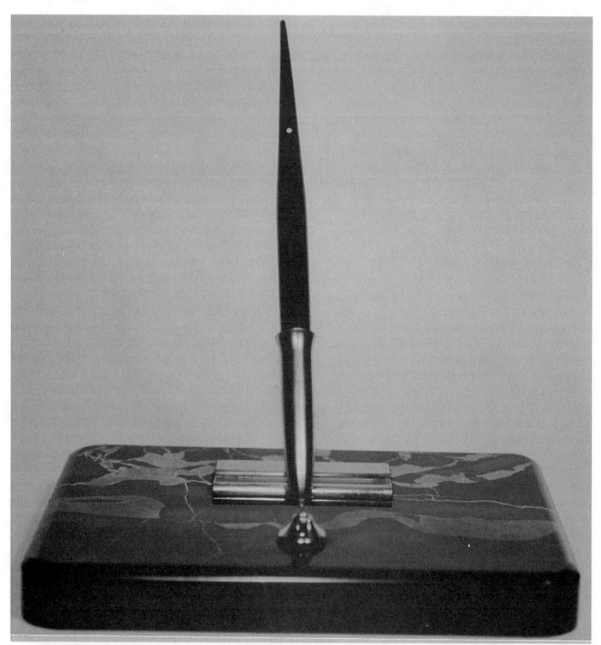

Onyx desk piece with brass plate penholder: $40.

Black glass desk piece with matching pen: $20.

Parker clock and double pen-catcher, 1930s: $300.

Single Wahl-Eversharp desk pen base. The base is onyx and the pen catcher is made of a wood-grained red and black hard rubber. 1920s: $40.

Single Wahl-Eversharp desk pen base. The pen catcher is hard rubber on a copper base: $35-$50 depending on size.

Desk piece with Shaeffer pen-catchers on white onyx, with pens $60, without pens, $25.

Distinctive Art Deco desk pen base and holder made of light bronze and black hard rubber: $60.

Black and green pearl pen catcher on black and white marble base, Wahl-Eversharp: $35.

Unmarked gold pen-catcher on golden onyx base: $15.

Stylistic Art Deco desk pen base and holder, similar to many Parker Pen Company products: $15.

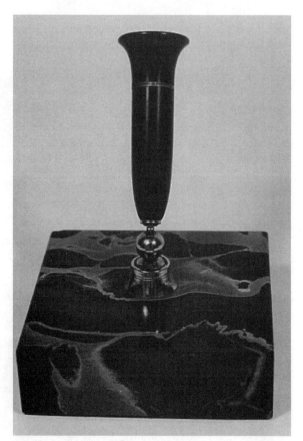

Black onyx base with a Sheaffer look-a-like pen-catcher: $10.

Bronze full-figure dog similar to those often found on more detailed inkwells. Black marble base with hammered brass pen-catcher: $180.

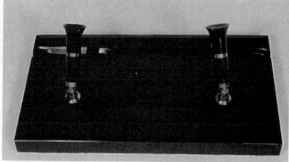

Double Sheaffer desk piece. Pen-catchers are coded for red and black ink, the one for red ink has a red band around its top: $68.

Twin Scottie dogs on green onyx pen-rest: $80.

Animals were a popular theme on many desk pen stands, as they had been on inkwells and inkstands before. Bronze horse on wood base with plastic pen catcher: $15-$20.

Dogs were especially popular on desk sets. A dog of unknown variety decks this piece: $10.

An elegant transitional piece from the period when inkwell molds were re-tooled to include a pen-catcher: 5 inches by 9 inches in bronze: $325.

SCHOOL PENS

A huge number of cheap, sturdy pens were produced for the school child upon graduation from the inkwell-in-the-desk dip-pen stage. These pens were taken upwards into the high school grades and even into college. They are plentiful and usually not worth much more than $1 to $2. Names might range from Wearever to Cardinal, Ritefine to Dependo. St. Louis maker Lipic, and the old Cross Pen Company, still in business, produced somewhat more valued lines. Cross products are notable due to their slim, slender length. Some of these had 14 karat nibs, which are always clearly marked.

There are several reference books on antique fountain pens which will yield more information about unusual pens, as well as the fancier varieties not often seen in the usual cigar box collection.

CHAPTER 7

DESK SETS AND ACCESSORIES

Desk sets and accessories were originally more popular and widespread in the halls of business than they were in the private home. Later Victorian days however, saw a wide variety of elegant desk accessories being offered by jewelers, catalogs, and large concerns such as Sears. Collectibles from this group include:

Pen-stands

Paperweights

Pen-trays

Desk and hand blotters

Rulers

Stamp containers

Desk lamps

Calendars

Magnifiers

Paperclips and spindles

Pencils

Pen-wipers

Erasers

Ink and ink containers

A typical 1930s desk setting. Bronze inkstand by Parker Pen Company features bronze over wood — rare to find one with calendar and ink stopper: $450. The carved wood elephant served as a paperweight: $50.

DESK SETS

Complete desk sets are not only difficult to locate, but almost impossible to complete. A basic set included only the necessities: an inkwell or stand, a desk blotter with decorative corner pieces, a separate rocker blotter, and a desk calendar.

More elaborate sets included as many as twenty separate pieces. In addition to the basic items, a photograph frame, a letter holder, a pounce holder (in older sets), a pen tray, and a paper knife or letter opener might have been included. Desk boxes for holding small items were also popular. Originally these boxes might have held sealing wax, and in later years, stamps. A stiff hog-bristle brush with a holder might also be encountered in larger desk sets. The brush was used to clean ink from pen nibs. The most elaborate sets even included a desk lamp, such as those produced by Tiffany. In fifteen years of searching, we have been able to

find only five or six sets that included more than four or five matched pieces.

In a lighter mood this 8 piece Victorian set would grace a lady's desk or a man's study with equal elegance. The early 1900s automobile paper clip to the right, is not part of the set. Blotter corners still firmly hold the original blotter pad securely: Set $1200. Individually the 4-cornered blotter $190, rocker blotter $140, letter opener $85, desk box $130, inkwell $350.

This Tiffany seven piece desk set is truly representative of the artistic detail produced by Tiffany studios in the early years of the century. Of the pine needle design each piece is marked "Tiffany Studios, New York." Glass of the highly prized green shade underlies the bronze spider webbing on the calendar frame, inkwell, desk box, and handle of the letter opener. When backlit this set glows with unbelievable lambency. Seven piece set would be priced at $6000 and up in such condition. Individually the blotter ends $450, box $750, frame $795, pentray $600, letter opener $425, inkwell $1250-$1500.

Set of dark bronze floral blotter corners in classic urn and foliage design popular from 1880-1890. Ball feet are required for these delicately worked bronze pieces: $325.

Egyptian desk set in dark bronze and gold plate, probably from the era of the opening of King Tutankhamen's tomb in the early 1920s. The massive yet graceful pieces resemble Tiffany's work, yet are uncataloged as such. Such pieces were often produced on special order and never reached production. The gold plated scarabs add brilliance and interest to the dark-end bronze pieces with this lotus and solar-winged design. Truly fit for a Pharaoh! Set: $5000. Individually: Tray, $350, letter opener, $250, paper clip, $375, desk box, $295, calendar frame, $280, rocker blotter, $250-$275, inkwell, $600.

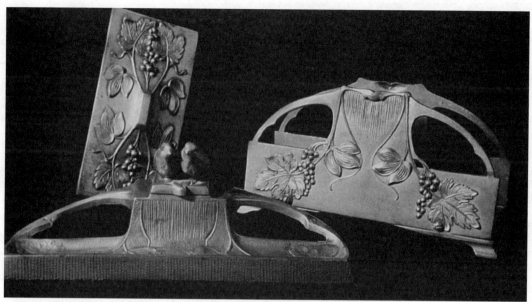

French 19th century light bronze three-piece set. This set accompanied a university professor to this country in 1893 and was still in the possession of his son (also a university professor), when sold in 1985. The epitome of the Art Nouveau naturalistic era, the grape and vine motif is charming and the lovebirds on the inkwell are exquisite. The unusually designed inkwell conceals two cobalt blue glass inserts. Set $3500-$5000. Inkwell $2000, rocker blotter $400, letter rack $750.

Bright brass set of 1930s vintage reflects the Art Deco styling that was prevalent in the 1920s and 1930s. Set $250. Cone inkwell $65, rocker blotter $30, frame $40, letter rack $20, desk brush & pen cleaner $20.

Three pieces in romantic brass. The elaborate scrolling ties them together as companion pieces. Rocker blotter $85, letter opener $75, paperweight $30. Courtesy E. Sargent.

Set of three desk pieces in pewter with such interesting styling that it would be a shame if a matching inkwell never turned up. Pen tray $75-$90, rocker blotter $70, pen brush and holder (to catch ink drips and clean nibs) $55.

DESK-BOXES, FILES, AND CADDIES

Desk-boxes and caddies served as mini-desks, containing spaces for pens, ink bottles and wells, paperclips, and other small items. Made of wood, these attractive and serviceable items helped keep desk clutter to a minimum. Small desk-boxes also served as travel desks, conveniently carrying the necessary writing accessories in a portable container.

Desk-top file sorters allowed the user to have current files at hand, yet still kept out of the way and neatly sorted. File-sorters usually had shelves which slid in and out, allowing easy access to needed materials.

This counter-top desk was produced by Sheaffer Pen Co. for its distributors. The writing surface is leather. A brass strip holds a pen from rolling down the slight slant. A deler name-plate is seen on the backboard, and a nicely placed ink bottle holder completes the writing-surface.

Rarely seen outside of a speciality store, these counter pieces can run upwards of $2.00.

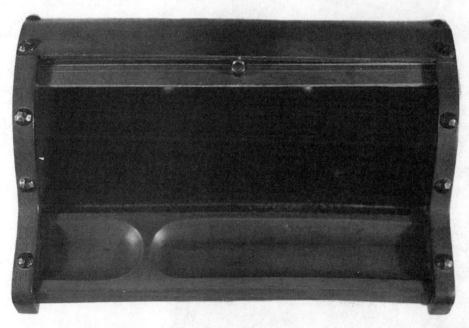

This rosewood desk caddy was produced c.1900-1915 for a home-office. It contained room for inkbottles, boxes of pen nibs, and other small office items. Two shallow wells held pens, pencils, and early paperclips. Rolltop-styling is rare and difficult to locate. Such an item might range from $600-1000, in this condition.

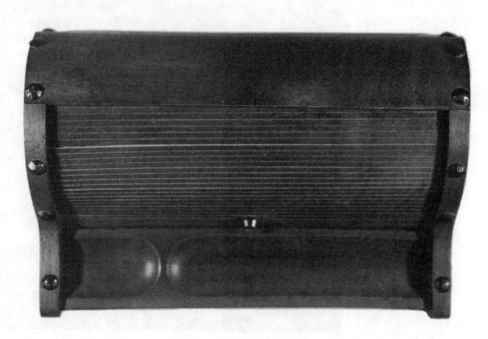

Desk-caddy with the rolltop closed. A small brass thumblift rolls up the cover into the cavity at the top. Measures 20 inches wide by 24 inches deep by 12-1/2 inches high.

153

A rolltop file-sorter with slide-in shelves to separate the files. Large files, such as legal folders or 11 x 14 inch folders, could be stored on the bottom. A brass thumb-lift lifts the rolltop back into the cavity at the top. An even more scarce item than the rolltop desk unit, these fileboxes, in rosewood or fir, and in this condition, bring $700 and up at auction.

An older desk box that might have been used as a travel desk as well. The hinged top sections open separately, to reveal inkwells for red and black ink, and a shallow tray to hold pens, etc. Decals on the corners are easily visible. Often found for $250 to $350, depending on condition.

BLOTTERS

Blotting paper, a thick spongy paper, acts as an absorbent for excess ink. In the 1500s, a thick paper covering was available for writing surfaces, but it was only a cousin to the modern blotter. Modern blotting paper, an accidental by-product of pulp milling, was invented in the 1800s. When rag was available, it was often added to the blotter "stew" to make a more absorbent product. Blotters were eventually found on nearly every desk, and became an effective advertising medium.

Rocker blotters predate the larger desk-pad blotter. They have a curved bottom portion of wood in older models and metal in more recent styles. A small strip of blotting paper was attached to the bottom. The blotter was then

Black elephant rocker blotter in glass. These 3 inch to 4 inch glass blotters are found in five or six basic shapes including a rocking horse, sailboat, and Scottie dog. Colors range from black to a rare lavender example: $40-$70.

Light pine wood box with glass lid contains a glass well, a rocker blotter, a quill knife, and a steel point dip-pen on lift out tray: $95.

155

Sober, businesslike 8 inch by 3 inch bronze blotter: $35.

European bronze-work rocker blotter. Very unusual design of peasants frolicking outdoors. Some suggest the design is reminiscent of Queen Marie Antoinette's garden parties at the Tuilleries where courtiers in white wigs dressed as peasants. This has not been proven, but the blotter is assuredly very old: $150.

A very 1930s product with an ingenious 50 year calendar — early computer technology. The desk pieces in white onyx are worth $35-40 each.

Silver dogwood floral set in Victorian type high relief. Double inkwell with hinge-back reveals two white porcelain wells when opened. $250 set. Inkwell $230, rocker blotter with flower knob $50-$75.

157

rocked back and forth to absorb the excess ink on freshly written pages. Made of wood, metal, glass, and plastic, these desk accessories are highly collectible. Many had figural tops; animal themes were especially popular. Others had intricate carving or pressed-in relief designs on their sides. A small number of colored glass rocker blotters in the shape of animals were produced in the 1930s and are highly prized by glass collectors as well as blotter collectors. Some are marked USA on the bottom, and at least one has been found with the capital I mark of the Imperial Glass Company. The forms range from dogs to sailboats, and may be found in black, green, yellow, cobalt, and white glass.

An iron "hand" paper-clip from the 1880s: $40.

This elaborate paper or mail sorter has "hands" that act as paper clips: $40.

PAPERCLIPS AND SPINDLES

Paperclips were standardized in the 1940s, replacing all varieties of "hand-shaped" clips and spring-loaded clasps, which abounded before that time. Hand-shaped clips consisted of a metal hand with a spring at the wrist, which held the paper against a flat base.

An early solution to paper clutter was the sharp metal spike mounted on a base of wood known as a spindle. A spindle might be found on any business desk to keep order, but were much less common in the home.

PAPERWEIGHTS

Paperweights evolved from a simple clean chunk of rock to the highest form of art glass. Both antique and modern paperweights are highly prized. Astronomic prices are paid even for new art glass paperweights. Many of the most cleverly crafted older paperweights are

Stylized fish paperweight is a touch-lift — the fish can hold a stack of papers under its head. In bronze, 7 inches by 3 inches: $115.

traded only in special auctions at Sotheby's or Christie's.

A serviceable but overlooked type of paperweight found in a great number of sizes is the "Dreadnought" or "Admiral." Named because of its resemblance to the ironclad Merrimack and Monitor of Civil War days, these weights began appearing during or just after the war. We have heard no fewer than twenty names for these heavy but efficient paperweights. Always made of metal and rarely marked, they may be found priced at only ten or twenty dollars in some shops – a real bargain price for desk accessories of such age.

Millefiore, an Italian term meaning "a thousand flowers," has been a popular style for

Art glass hollow sphere with flat base paperweight. Gold and blue enamel overlay 3-7/8 inches: $80.

Two examples of the dreadnought style paperweight said to resemble an ironclad warship. On the left foreground is a small 3 inch example. Most are made of oval shaped iron, but some are round. Many have raised-letter advertising or a logo glued to their base: $40. On the right is a much larger "dreadnought" in dull-finished iron. These iron weights are extremely heavy and not well balanced. Many iron companies produced them: $50.
In the rear is a soapstone inkwell: $85-$100.

Group of "end of day" paperweights whose design is created by a bubble of colored glass within the clear overlay. Prices range from $25 up, depending on design. Far right is of a different "bubble" type: $50.

glass paperweights. The weights are made from bundles of thin rods of colored glass, which are fused together and cut into sections. The thin rods are arranged in such a way that they look like flowers in cross section. These flowers rise from the depths of the base and are encased inside a round glass dome.

Bronze bell weight 3-7/8 inches high: $40, brass anvil $30.

Millefiore weights were produced in Europe, especially Italy, for hundreds of years. Made by highly skilled glass artisans, most of these weights are unmarked. Modern styles of millefiore have been produced in Japan. Of less elaborate design, even these paperweights have a high value.

Because of their beauty and popularity, many millefiore weights have been reproduced. Great care must be taken to buy them only from a knowledgeable source or do a great deal of reading so that you'll be making an informed purchase – Caveat Emptor.

"Little Mermaid" tourist piece from Copenhagen. These have been produced for over 75 years. $60.

Art Deco girl in clinging teddy on onyx base, 5 inches high: $75 and up.

Scottie in alloy metal. 8 inches by 7-3/4 inches: $50.

Greyhound-type dog in bronze on onyx base. 7-3/4 inches by 8 inches: $50.

Large Borzoi paperweight on slab of interesting metamorphic stone. The green of the hound, sparked with gold, dates it to 1920-26. 8 inches by 10 inches: $150.

Linear flattened brass hunting dog on point: $30.

Brass full-form lion on rock 1920s: $55.

Left: Sleek shark in brass: $45 Right: Turtle's shell is hinged, opening to a compartment for storing paper clips: $30.

Bronze elephant with realistic detailing hails from 1880-1890. Naturalistic period. 9 inches: $200.

Group of three paperweights.
Left: Brass owl on onyx: $25.
Center: Unusual pewter personalized piece marked "J. Crow Taylor, Journalist, Louisville, KY." An unusual play on names: $80.
Right: Pelican on onyx: $35.

PENCILS

Pencils of unusual style and color, as well as those made as matching pieces by one of the major pen companies, are most collected. The most desirable are automatic pencils of several special types Advertising pencils with old gas station or out-of-business shoe store names are extremely popular. Another type has an oil-filled clear section in the middle of the pencil containing floating figures. A rare example of this type features a tiny girl wearing a bathing suit and advertises the Jantzen Swimsuit Company. A full collection can be made of these pencils with clear barrels containing dice, figurines, shoes, boats, and other figures.

Another collectible type of pencil is the "bullet" pencil. A short pencil fits into a metal

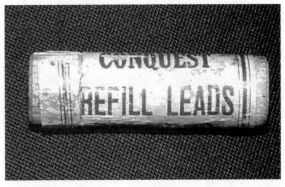

Associational items, such as this container for pencil leads, add a nice touch to a collection and are still quite affordable. Conquest Pencil Lead Refill: $3.

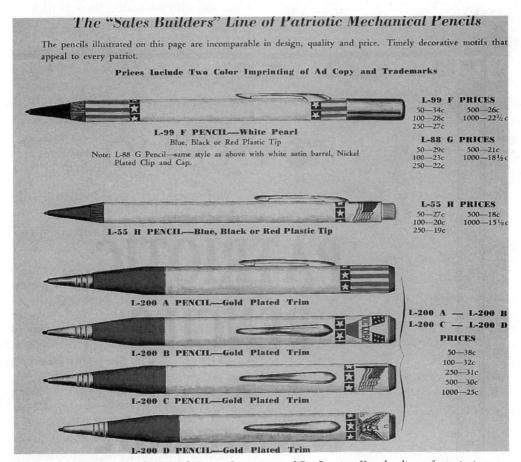

During World War II, the Joseph Lipic Company of St. Louis offered a line of patriotic pencils. The pencils were given away with the purchase of each war bond. (Catalog page courtesy Leonard Lipic.)

holder and is covered by a bullet-shaped metal cap, which protects the lead when the pencil is not in use. Bullet pencils are almost always advertising pieces, given away as promotions.

Older automatic pencils were made of silver, sterling silver, or gold. It is unusual to find these pencils at all, let alone in good condition. They do exist, however, and may be reconditioned and used, or displayed as a cherished keepsake.

INK BOTTLES

Ink bottles and containers began to be common in the early 1800s and may form a separate collection. These bottles may be collected for many reasons – age, color, out-of-business makers, older box, and bottle styles. Some collections consist of all the colors of ink produced by a single ink maker.

First produced in stoneware crocks and jugs, bottles of these materials continued to be produced until late Victorian times. Many are marked with names on the bottom, or on paper labels that may have partially or wholly dissolved off the container. Of all sizes from few spoonfuls to a quart or more, these ink containers make a fascinating study and an interesting collection.

Master ink bottles were large bottles, usually about two pints, which were used to fill smaller inkbottles and wells. Usually made of ironstone, they were a necessity in schools and business offices. If found with pouring spout intact and with ink inside, these bottles command high prices.

Glass bottles for ink have been produced for hundreds of years. Of these, blown glass models from colonial times are especially popular. They may be recognized, like other blown glass items, by the pontil mark on the bottom. Some manufacturers impressed their names and perhaps their trademarks on the bottom or side of the bottle, but many are unmarked.

Most sought are purple bottles that were originally clear glass. Colored by a reaction of the minerals in the glass to sunlight, these bottles are most often found in abandoned towns and desert areas. Other desirable bottle colors include cobalt blue, teal, aqua, showy greens, black, yellow, and finally brown and clear.

The most wanted shapes are the figural: houses, animals, shoes, and heads. Collectors also covet bottles with pen rests molded into the glass. An unusual "umbrella" bottle in an octagon shape, usually found in light green, is also a rare find

Glass inkbottles are often found lurking amongst dusty patent medicine bottles. Glass bottle shows are fine places to locate them.

Two examples of master ink bottles:
Left: Master ink with pour cap, which was packed in box separately: $20. With both caps: $25.
Right: Sanford "Ink for office and Library" often had corks. This cork has a center hole as it was used to ink stamp pads and flow was cut down to a trickle: $40-$50.

INKS

A collection may also be made of the varying types of pen-makers' particular inks such as Skrip and Quink.

Although most pen-makers eventually settled on blue-black as the color of choice, red, green, and even purple inks reached popularity in the years since fountain pens were first produced. Old pens often yield inks of decidedly unusual colors when soaked to clean their nibs. Old ink can be used in fountain pens if it has never been opened. If it has been opened, the ink should be strained through a cloth and then poured back into the bottle.

Ink collectors are found in every country. One of the best known is Masa Sunami of Japan, whose extensive collection only partially survived after a disastrous earthquake in the region several years ago.

Japanese ink bottle with an unusual lid. Courtesy M. Sunami.

A trio of 1920s ink bottles. Carter led the ink field for almost 30 years: $5 each.

167

Evolution of Carter ink styles from their inception to the 1940s: $7-$8 each.

Left: Parker advertised "Super Chrome" as a fast drying ink for the blotter-less age: $7-$10 each if labels and caps are clean.
Center: A later Sheaffer Skrip bottle which actually uses the word "ink" – for years Sheaffer only referred to Skrip as a "writing fluid." $2.
Right: Attractive Carter's Ink bottle with sea gull design on label: $5-10.

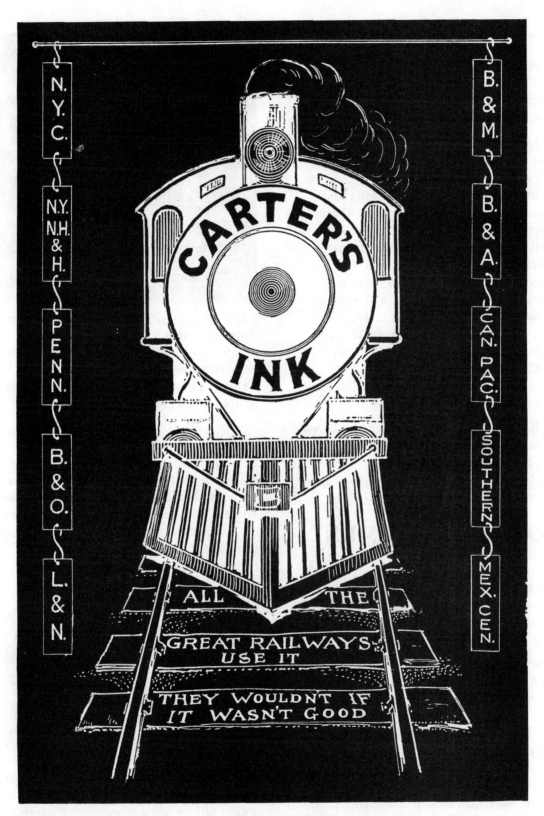

Carter's Ink advertisement from 1899. The rare "pufferbelly" train engine gives this ad crossover appeal to railroad collectors. Munsey's Magazine ad page: $4-$8.

BOOKENDS

Antique bookends make an attractive and functional addition to any desk. They are most commonly made of wood, pot metal, bronze, brass, chalkware, and glass.

Like inkwells, the styles of bookends have often reflected artistic movements of the day such as Art Nouveau and Art Deco. Roycroft, one of the better-known Arts &Crafts firms, produced several styles of bookends. Often sculptural in quality, bookends can be almost bewildering in their variety. Popular themes include ships, people, animals, and mythological figures. Glass horses were especially popular at one time, and were produced by several large glassmaking firms. More recently, pop culture icons have been portrayed on bookends. There is a highly desirable set of bookends formed of Elvis Presley from waist up with a guitar. The set was made of chalk, and dated 1977.

Bookends can either add much to your basic collection, or form a separate collection of their own. Not surprisingly, bookends are very popular among book collectors, and one may run into competition from these collectors.

OFFICE EQUIPMENT

Even office items once regarded as strictly utilitarian are being bought up by collectors. Typewriters and typewriter ribbon tins are among the most popular of these items.

Typewriters were first commercially manufactured in the 1870s. Within a decade they were widely used in business offices. There was much variety in design of these early machines, and collectors are most interested in these models. Early models, usually finished with glossy black enamel, were often embellished with pinstripes or other decorative flourishes. By the 1920s, model designs had become more standardized. These later typewriters are generally less desirable to collectors. Some exceptions from later decades

Older manual typewriter by L.C. Smith Company There are many sorts of typewriters, the earliest may not even look like a typewriter, so care should be taken to find out what the office item might be. This model is from about 1935, and quite common: $50. Courtesy Leslie Haltbakk.

do pique collector interest. Several portable machines, produced in the 1920s, were issued in the bright Art Deco inspired colors of the time. Some of the early electric models, before these too became standardized, are also quite sought after. Today, as the computer has almost completely replaced the typewriter, interest in

Four wax-stamp seals. These range from family crests to flower symbols to names or initials. Of ancient heritage, these examples are a mere 80 years old. Hard to price: $15-$20 for the brass examples, $35-$50 for the wood.

these older machines is sure to increase among collectors.

Ribbons used to ink typewriters were often sold in decorative tins. Smaller and easier to store than the machines themselves, these tins have become popular with many collectors. Rectangular, round and square in shape, typewriter tins were lithographed with colorful scenes. Animals, ships, airplanes, birds, women, flowers, and cars are some of the most popular designs.

The earliest tins date from the 1890s. Tins were used to package typewriter ribbons into the 1960s, when cardboard and plastic became more cost effective. Well known for their inks, Carter's became a major supplier of typewriter ribbons. Many typewriter makers, such as Remington, Corona, L.C. Smith, and Oliver, also sold "house brand" ribbons. The bottom of the tin was stamped with the models with which the ribbon was compatible. Some collectors may concentrate on the tins for a particular model of

typewriter, while other collections may be based on the ribbon manufacturer, the city of manufacture, or the design on the tin.

After the ribbon was used, the decorative tin was usually kept as a handy container for paperclips, tacks, hairpins, or spare change. Because they were not often thrown out, typewriter tins are quite readily found today, usually for reasonable prices.

Other office equipment prized by collectors include calendars, adding machines and calculators, desk lamps, letter boxes, magnifying glasses, file cabinets, and traveling desks. Few books are available on most of the items, but careful study of old catalogs and reference books will provide some needed information and perhaps a few clues to their age and maker.

Since these are new collecting fields as inkwells and fountain pens were only a few decades ago, the field is wide open and pricing varies greatly.

The salesman's best friend, a traveling desk. Designed for use on a train or early passenger plane this 15 inch by 9 inch piece features a leather covered fold-out blotter and pockets, a pen-rest, pen and tool box, and a double-snap hinge inkwell. A jewel of design and utterly rare to locate: $350.

Typewriter tin made by "Codo" company of Chicago. Plainer tins such as this example range from: $4-7.

Reverse side of Codo tin — contained ribbon for L.C. Smith and Smith Corona models.

More attractive typewriter tins, such as this 1960s tin with a Japanese flower arrangement, range from: $5-$15.

Another attractive typewriter tin, this one with a Greek motif of Diana the Huntress: $10-15.

Carter's made typewriter ribbons, as well as inks. Carter's Midnight ribbons were quite popular and the tins are quite plentiful even today: $5-8.

Type Bar typewriter tin made for, and by, Smith Corona. An extremely popular ribbon in its day, these tins are quite common and only valued at: $2-4.

A 1930's adding machine. These machines are often interesting and complex and almost all of them still work! This one requires a two-toned inked ribbon, black and red, which may be hard to find in our computer age: $45. Some of the older models may bring several hundred dollars.

FOR THE OFFICE

82

Only Machine

Which will add all the columns at a time.

That foots scattered items and cross footings as well as regular columns.

Which will perform Multiplication or Division or Compute interest by Automatic keys.

Operated by keys which actually does the carrying from one column to all the others.

Absolutely accurate, and twice as quick as the best accountant.

Saving the hours and days spent in looking for mistakes in taking trial balances.

EVER INVENTED

No Agents.   Write for pamphlet.

FELT & TARRANT MFG. CO. 52–56 Illinois Street, Chicago.

The "Comptometer" was an early adding machine. The advent of "scientific management" and industrialization made machines like this more prevalent in office and shops in the late 1800s. This page from an 1893 issue of Century magazine also advertises other items for the office.

A NEW INVENTION.

THE
Simplex Printer

100 copies of any writing or drawing in twenty minutes.
This is a new apparatus for duplicating copies
of writings or drawings.

It is the cleanest, cheapest and simplest, as well as the most reliable, duplicating apparatus in existence. Requires no washing; any boy can work it.

From an original, on any ordinary paper, with any pen, 100 copies can be made; or, with an original, written on the typewriter, 50 copies can be produced, quickly and without trouble, in 15 minutes.

The simplicity and ease with which copies of letters, circulars, price-lists, examination papers, drawings, specifications, music etc., can be reproduced in various colors at one operation makes it invaluable.

Agents wanted everywhere. Send for circulars and samples of work.

LAWTON & CO., 20 Vesey Street, New-York.

An early copier. The Simplex printer took only twenty minutes to make 100 copies — and required no washing!

Related objects such as this 1910-check protector can add to an office or desk collectibles collection. This unique example is 3 inches in diameter and is valued at $45 to $75. It pierced holes in paper to protect a check. Other check protectors in heavy cases with letters and handles can range in price from $75 to $200 and are now very hard to find in working condition.

The 1890s Hammond typewriter looks quite different from our modern notion of typewriters and word processors.

This 1892 Century Magazine page had ads for four different typewriter companies on the same page!

The real mystery stands up. This common office piece, often labeled and sold as an inkwell, has inspired correspondence in more than one journal of inkwell collectors – not to mention at antique shows and sales exhibits. The seller will stoutly maintain that it IS an inkwell, while the customer says NOT. It is and it isn't. A glue company distributed the apparatus. One theory suggests that it was used to apply a drop of glue to a non-glue ready envelope. Other theories maintain that it was used to put one drop of ink onto a stamp or pen. As the '60s song goes, "I never knew just what it was, and I guess I never will." Value of $25-50 if label is intact.

CHAPTER 8

ADVERTISING ITEMS

The field of advertising collectibles is large, ranging from old-time advertisers' trade cards to actual items sold by the companies involved. Competition for everything pertaining to certain manufacturers is fierce, and thousands may be paid for a stick of "coke" gum or a certain type of 1920s gasoline pump. And yet, there are certain categories of advertising collectibles, still available if not plentiful, which are virtually ignored by the collecting public.

One of the most important factors in business success is keeping the name or symbol of the company in the view of the consumer. Trillions of dollars are spent every year in the pursuit of customer-recognition factor.

In the days before television, advertisers seized upon radio as a potentially fantastic medium for selling their products. Early advertis-

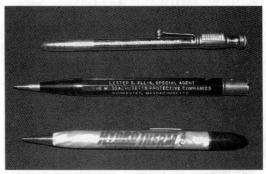

Trio of advertising pencils. The top example has an unusual clip which contains a small calendar dating from January 1915. The center pencil was a give-away from a Massachusetts insurance company. The bottom example was given by a New Jersey heating company — the "bullet" on the end conceals an eraser. Prices range from $5-20.

ing was chattier and less glossy than the sleek special-effects-ridden-spectaculars of today. Even

A fine example of a drug company Lucite ball paperweight. This one was given to introduce Inderal, a blood pressure medication more than 20 years ago: $45-$60.

Lucite block ad paperweight is desirable both as an advertising item and a sports collectible: $35-$55. If scratched or blurred, price drops drastically.

A copper gasoline station desk piece. Pegasus was an early Mobil gasoline icon. Fine condition: $90.

Perpetual calendar desk piece produced for Kiwanis Clubs in the early 1920s and 1930s: $70 and up.

before radio, the importance of the sales-stimulator was well known. A sales- stimulator is any item that is given away as a prize, premium, or keepsake.

In this category are a plethora of office products, which could be imprinted in one way or another with the name of the company involved. This practice is still followed although the range of imprinted items has narrowed to some degree. Early gifts presented to the customer at holiday times include penholders into which a steel pen point might be inserted, calendars, blotters, rulers, pencils, letter openers, paperweights, clocks, desk calendars, appointment books, memo holders, telephone dialers and other desk equipment. By presenting an item both useful and decorative, with the proper advertising included, the producer could accomplish his purpose.

In time, huge companies sprang up designed only to produce these advertising specialties, and many are still happily producing much the same type of items for office use which were given in late Victorian times. Several hundred types of ballpoint pens exist, which are produced by the hundreds of thousands to be given in the same way that a simple wooden pencil may have been in 1867.

Few are the businesses and homes that do not receive at least one advertising calendar in the holiday mail, all bearing gorgeous photographs, artwork, and, prominently, the name of the giver. Whether the offering is hung upon the wall or thrown out is often left to chance, but the thought is the same, as is the purpose.

Early sales stimulators are highly collectible, no matter their age or condition. Specialized categories exist in which the productions of

This 1941 gravity well recorded the 50th anniversary of a St. Louis electric company. Employees as well as clients probably received one: $85-$95.

Attractive desktop pen holder and calendar commemorated the 150th anniversary of the Phoenix Insurance Company. The piece dates from the 1930s and was probably given away to employees and valued customers. In bronze: $30-40.

a well-known company may be worth many times more than a lesser-known company. This explains why the ferocious market exists for anything given away by the Coca-Cola Company. Coca-Cola premiums are the subject of many books and price guides, as are others in

the high-end category. Yet there is a wide and fertile field of collectibility in the gifts and premiums of literally thousands of less famous producers.

Of course, the collector may prefer to align himself with those who are interested only in a single company or type of product, such as beer, sewing threads, ink, or automobiles to mention a few.

If the collector becomes more interested in the type or product rather than the brand names involved, there is wider selection and availability. If you collect lithographed ink blotters of any of a variety of sorts, you will find a more varied choice offered than if you narrow your field of interest to only blotters produced by insurance companies, for instance.

A collector who is new to the field may choose one of several options. You may select a category of items and concentrate only on those, without regard to which company's name may appear on them. Secondly, you might wish to specialize in a certain company's output although that may limit your choice in number if

Lithographed paper blotters were an inexpensive and effective advertising medium. Elizabeth's Poultry Farm blotter: $7-$9.

Blotter with 2 collectibility aspects: as a blotter and also as related to early bottling for soda and beer 1915: $12-$14.

Another blotter from the Loew Manufacturing Company with double value: $15

Another look at Loew Manufacturing equipment: $15.

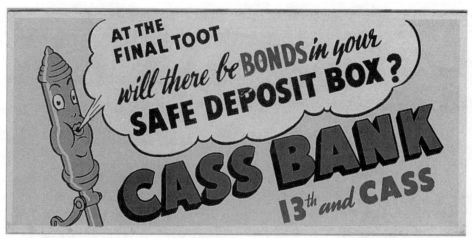

Commercial ad blotter for Cass Bank: $9-$11.

not quality. It is wise to carefully consider both of these options before making a decision.

There is a further factor to consider. Even if you intend eventually to concentrate upon things produced by, for instance, Ford Motor Company, you may want to collect what is presented to you at a reasonable price; even if an item does not fit into that special category, it might prove of great value at a later time. Although Ford might be your own goal, the Quaker Oats Company item that you purchased might be just the item another collector might be willing to trade for his Ford Motor Company paperweight. Therefore, it is a good idea not to pass over a good buy in vintage advertising even if it does not have the logo of the company you prefer. We have always followed this rule and it has proven

Associated collectibles, such as this Esterbrook's printing block, may be of value if they feature pens, nibs, ruler, or inkwells 4 inches by 2 inches: $45-60.

of value to us many times in providing good bartering items.

There is a wide selection of advertising items ranging from those actually used in or associated with the act of writing, to items which could be found on any businessman's desk. Some of the most available items, still underpriced in most cases yet potentially able to form the basis of a fine collection, include:

Company letterhead also makes a unique and interesting addition to a collection.

Old magazine advertisements can add a nice touch to a collection, and are quite affordable. This Waterman ad from 1919 shows the company's New York City headquarters: Harper's Magazine page: $1.

Waterman's Ideal Fountain Pen

The Most Important Part Of Your Vacation Outfit

THERE is nothing more necessary to the convenience of those who travel than a reliable fountain pen. Remember that it is the superior writing qualities of Waterman's Ideals that will serve you best. Wherever you go take your Waterman's Ideal, and you will at once appreciate that your letters home and friendly post cards can be written with the ease and comfort for which present day pen making has proficiently provided.

Booklet on Request

Our Safety Pen

is made to carry in any position you want to. It can roll around in your grip or trunk and cannot spill. The barrel is sealed by the cap (as illustrated). The gold pen screws out into place for writing by a simple little twist, when the cap is off.

All Dealers

Avoid Imitations and Substitutes

L. E. Waterman Co., 173 BROADWAY, NEW YORK

8 School St., Boston - 189 Clark St., Chicago - 734 Market St., San Francisco - 123 St. Francois Xavier St., Montreal - 12 Golden Lane, London

Another Waterman ad, this one for a black hard rubber "safety" pen. McClure's Magazine *page from 1910: $2.*

Wooden rulers	Wooden pencils
Early ballpoint pens	Penknives
Quill cutters	Letter openers
Lithographed blotters	Rocker blotters
Wall calendars	Desk calendars
Paperweights	Business cards
Desk diaries	Desk boxes
Fountain pens	Ink-holders (all types)
Check writing equipment	Matched desk sets
Appointment books	Erasers
Ink bottles (all types)	Steel pen nibs
Notebooks	Memo holders
Novelty items such as very large pencils	Automatic pencils
Writing memorabilia such as Palmer writing method manuals	Magazine ads

Within each category, there are smaller categories such as those items produced only by a certain company over a period of decades, and subject-categories such as "pinup girl" calendars. In many antique stores and malls, a large part of the above list is not only present, but also underpriced. You will discover a broad selection in many categories, smaller in others that have already become popular collectibles.

We have always followed a policy of asking the shop owner if he or she has any of the items we seek before spending time rummaging on our own. It is also a good idea to introduce yourself with a small business card or a plain index card with your name, phone number, and short list of items you are seeking. Most antique dealers are genuinely interested in helping you to find items you seek, and will probably keep your "wants" on file for future use.

In several of these categories, there is a trade publication with ads and perhaps articles on the history of the item. Many of these will be listed at the rear of this book.

A specialized writing implement store as it would have looked in the 1940s. Old advertising displays and store fixtures are very collectible, and make excellent displays for vintage pen collections.

COMMERCIAL PENS

Although not plentiful, a small number of fountain pens were produced as advertising giveaways or attention-grabbers on confectionery countertops.

These will include the Pepsi-Cola fountain pen in the traditional red, white and blue, the elusive and rare Coca-Cola pen, the Mickey Mouse pen complete with ears, and the super-hero lines from Superman to Dick Tracy.

These pens were cheaply made, but were undeniably sturdy as a number of them remain. Prices range from $25 to $50 for a clean, unbroken example.

The Peter Pan pen is in this category, although it is a miniature pen and likely to be decorated with plastic or celluloid flowers in unlikely places. Usually pastel, they are appealing to youngsters and to some female collectors.

The Shirley Temple pen set was produced in the pre-war years and bears her name on nib and barrel. Mostly found in green, the other colors are rarer and correspondingly pricier as they are attractive not only to Shirley collectors but pen collectors as well.

Local pens were produced, commemorating anything from the Statue of Liberty to baseball heroes. These pens also command more attention as a double attraction to more than one group of collectors.

LETTER OPENERS

Letter openers, which were born when the gummed envelope became common and the wax seal disappeared, joined the ranks of advertising sales stimulators somewhere in the late 1880s. They too were items, which once given, would tend to stay on the desks of the recipients. Most were designed for a male audience—severe in styling and with little decoration. "Just the facts ma'am" was the idea. Although small company logos appeared on these early openers, usually only the business name and address, followed by

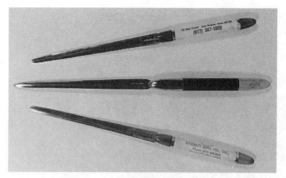

Three advertising letter openers carrying clear advertising messages on the handles: $25-$45.

a telephone number, if the town had telephones, were included. The majority of these openers bear the names of such emporiums as "Sam's Garage," or that of a gas and oil station. These were often given as Christmas gifts to holiday-time customers or mailed to a list of known clients. Letter openers of a finer quality represent those sent out by large corporations or given to employees as a holiday gift. Many of these are not elaborate and are understated in design.

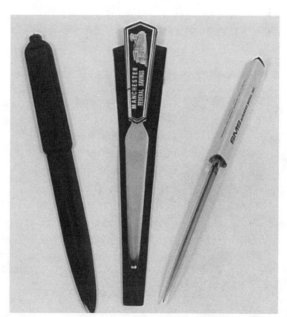

Three interesting advertising letter openers of various design.
The example in the center with sheath and raised design is very unusual: $40, others $20.

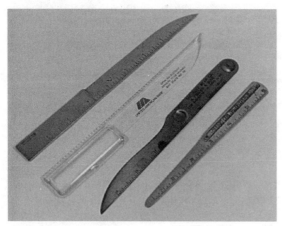

Group of ruler/letter openers, one of the most interesting triple collectibles as they offer ruler, letter opener, and advertising piece all in one package!

Left: Imprinted one piece steel from 1950's. Fine manufacture 9 inches: $60.

Center left: A Lucite ruler opener with bank advertising. 8 inches 1970's: $25.

Center right: Brass indented example from a baby-wear company, 1940's: $30-35.

Right: Imprinted steel ruler/opener with manufacturing company advertisement: $30.

The focus of advertising stimulators changed slightly in the 1920s when women's suffrage became the law of the land, and women began to drive automobiles and to take positions in business. Letter openers were adorned with more elaborate designs and were often formed of celluloid lace or catalin cast in Art Deco styles.

When the use of plastics became more prevalent, another change occurred and openers with a magnifying glass optical grinding appeared. A second category of openers with encased objects was also produced in plastic. Encased items ranged from a small lithograph to a four-leaf clover, and were sealed under small domes of clear isinglass or celluloid.

More recently, since 1945, figural letter openers made of plastic appeared. They usually feature a human or animal figure at the end opposite the point. Most common in this class are the letter openers of the Fuller Brush Company. Originally depicting a simple outline of the "Fuller Brush Man," the design evolved into a reversible opener that featured a male outline on one side and a female on the other. This dual-sex figure is the least common of the Fuller-

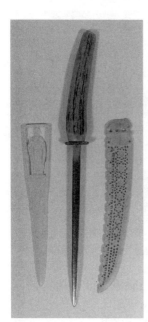

French ivory and horn openers.

Left: Combination bookmark and letter opener with Apostolic figure in French ivory (celluloid): $20.

Center: Horn forms a comfortable handle for this steel 8 inch blade: $60.

Right: Elephant-top lace of 1930's manufacture: $25.

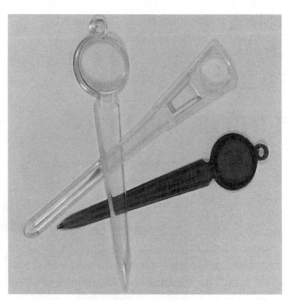

More recent plastic letter openers often feature magnifying lenses on the handle. These are not difficult to locate and cost $5 to $10.

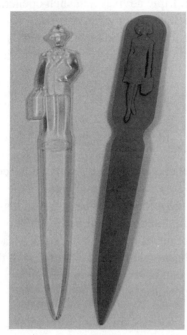

Two styles of Fuller Brush letter openers. On the right is the rarer opener with the woman on one side (shown) and the man on the reverse: $20.

Brush letter openers, and many advertising letter opener collectors prize it. All of the large corporations provided letter openers, from Coca-Cola and 7-Up to the staid and proper insurance companies whose offerings always looked expensive.

A fine collection may be built up with a little effort and the courage to ask the shop-owner or the garage-sale proprietor if they have any old letter openers for sale. These tend to stay in drawers for decades, and many fine examples still await the collector.

Side categories of openers include the souvenir type, which can be artistic and desirable, or gaudy and gauche. They are in the same materials as are the strictly trade-stimulating variety, ranging from metal to celluloid to today's plastics.

Their composition, their feel, and sometimes even their color can date plastics. At the end of World War II, a type of plastic was produced which was swirled with color like that of a marble. Dating can also be done by observing the evolution of telephone numbers from no numbers to four digits to seven digits and beyond. Zip codes are another method of dating, as they did not exist before WWII for the most part, and might have consisted of a single digit, such as "Springfield 6, Ohio."

Prices for letter openers have not yet been firmly established as far as advertising varieties are concerned. Victorian types are becoming not only rare, but extremely expensive and should be snapped up as fast as possible. Anyone with a

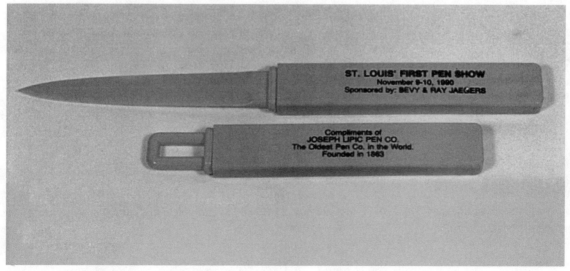

Two-piece letter opener made by the Joseph Lipic Pen Co. St. Louis Pen Show souvenir: $30.

189

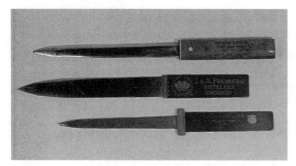

Group of knifelike letter openers with very sharp tips.
Top: Laminated wood handle with advertising for a lumberyard. 7-3/4 inches: $40.
Middle: All steel opener with seal of a distillery, which doubles its value, 8 inches: $70
Bottom: Wood, leather, and bone opener from a pharmaceutical company. 6 inches: $55

good eye can expect to assemble a fine advertising letter opener collection in a fairly short time.

By the way, the latest trend in letter openers for the business trade is the type produced by Lipic Pen Company of St. Louis, Missouri. In two pieces, one end opens to reveal the sharp point, and then becomes the handle when put back together. Lipic advises that such openers make a fine defense item when carried in a man's pocket, a child's book bag, or a lady's purse. In addition, it will also open your mail.

RULERS

Rulers, whether of wood, metal, celluloid, or plastic, are one of the most undiscovered of the writing-related categories. Available for centuries, they were made for commercial use beginning in the midpoint of the 1800s industrial revolution. Suddenly their use was not only as an article of measurement, but also as a trade-stimulator. The wooden ruler became one of the first and least expensive of the entire category of advertising specialties.

Children, students, and adults use rulers, making them the perfect vehicle for carrying an all-encompassing message through each generation of users. With the name "Putnam's Dyes" under your eyes every time you measured a hem or a linear inch, you could not forget the message. At the shop, you would naturally choose the dye in the Putnam box.

Very fine presentation business gift ruler still in original box. Lovely brass example with both types of measurement on opposite sides: $95-up.

Rulers were popular give-aways for many businesses. Made of inexpensive wood, they were useful items which customers tended to hold onto: $4-12 depending on condition and advertising.

Hardware stores and lumber companies seized upon the advertising ruler as the linear foot is their lifeblood even today, and gifted all comers with rulers, large and small. Even today, most larger hardware stores will present you with a yardstick bearing their trademark if you request one.

Wood lends itself perfectly to lithographing or imprinting with ink, an indelible method of advertising. Rulers may be found with logo or trademark, company name and address, and even artistic designs imprinted upon their surface. Most are made of cheap unvarnished pine, yet are of intense interest because of the immense variety of names of forgotten garages, laundries and other business, many of which are no longer in existence.

Rulers of higher quality might be of sturdier wood, with highly varnished surfaces, and imprints in gold leaf. Some are rigid, some may fold, and still others may have metal rims to assure a straight edge. Those with company names are as collectible as the less expensive variety.

Rulers may generally be dated by whether they are simply rules of the twelve-inch foot, or include the metric system as well, which was not common in this country until the 1970s.

Yardsticks, such as this give-away from Ace Hardware, were popular promotional items for hardware and dry goods stores. This example is lithographed on wood and painted, and dates form 1950s-1960s—before metrics were introduced to the U.S.: $5-10.

191

CHAPTER 9

RESTORATION AND REPAIR TIPS

There is an aphorism in the collectibles field involving the usual belief that antiques should not be repaired or restored. In this field of inkwells, pens and desk furnishings, this may be modified by the usage to which your items are to be put. If they are merely to be displayed and not used, then they should be interfered with as little as possible.

However, if you plan to use the item, for instance a pen you admire and wish to restore to its full potential as a writing instrument, then there is certainly nothing at all wrong with providing your antique with such repair that will restore it.

BROKEN PENS

Pens may have defects unknown to the dealer, but the most common defect is the lack of the nib, and the second would be a cap crack.

A cap crack was less common when the gold cap band entered the pen-making art, as this band was not only decorative, but reduced the number of cap cracks caused by overly-

An amateur should not attempt pen repair. Consult an expert who knows how these delicate old pens should be restored. If you use metal tools to open or repair a pen, the 'jaws' of the pliers MUST be covered in rubber hose cut to fit. For education and tips, consult Pen World Magazine. Courtesy Ray Call.

A broken and corroded pen nib such as this example, found on an inexpensive Wearever pen, is beyond repair.

Beneath each nib is a pellet of harder metal which is the only writing surface. A good nib must have the pellet intact.

ambitious pen-closings. Even a triple band, however, may not insure against a cap crack. Cap cracks may be located by gently inserting

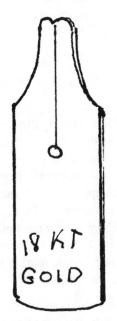

Nib tips must be gently rounded and even - never broken off.

the little fingertip into the cap of the pen and rotating the cap upon the fingertip, feeling for uneven surfaces. All the pens that you intend to offer for sale or to buy should be tested in this way, as well as with a lighted magnifier.

If a crack or known defect is observed, it does not mean the pen is worthless. It should, however, be marked "as is" so that the pen buyer will be aware of the defect. The price should be considered negotiable in these cases. You may just need the nib, or a feed section, to complete another pen.

PEN PARTS

Most fountain pen owners kept parts of pens, which did not work. Today, because most antique dealers do not realize that antique fountain pens can be repaired and restored, these parts may be thrown out as useless.

A usable selection of pen clips, feed sections, or other invaluable parts may be found in such ratty-looking collections. A team of enterprising young men was thinking along just

Auction finds such as this often come packaged in a colorful cigar box. A treasure may be lurking at the bottom, or it may yield useful replacement parts.

these lines a few years ago when they purchased restored and repaired a small factory where rubber ink sacs for pens had been made years ago. They even located some of the retired workers who had staffed the place, and learned the ins and outs of ink sac making. Today, they are the proud possessors of a thriving empire and the only source of ink sacs in America.

CARE AND FEEDING OF BLACK RUBBER PENS

Many people look at hard black rubber pens and believe they are made of some older type of plastic. Some of these have been left in sunlight and thus are brown instead of black. No hard rubber pens were made in brown, however, and those that seem to be brown are merely faded. Do NOT attempt to restore the black color to

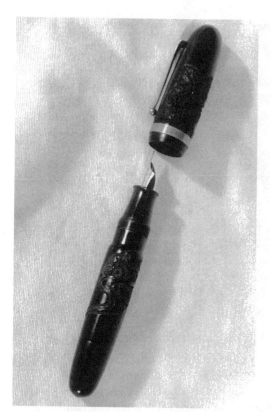

Hard black rubber pens must be treated gently - keep out of direct sunlight and do not use abrasive cleaners. This example is marked "J. Schnell" and has an attractive floral design. 6-1/2 inches long: $150 and up.

these pens, as an amateur cannot restore it to the original color.

It was thought that soaking these pens in bleach would restore them to their original glossy luster, but this treatment is not recommended as it also makes the pen's surface fuzzy and blurred in appearance. It may cause long term damage to the pen and will also ruin the gold-filled, gold-washed or gold plated trim. If the pen is not to be sold, but kept for personal use, a black permanent magic marker may be carefully used to restore the color.

Rubber pens may also be restored to a shiny luster by rubbing a tiny amount of very thin sewing machine or 3-in-1 oil into the surface with a scrap of flannel.

Gold trim or covering may be gently polished with a jewelry polishing cloth, and some types can be burnished with a dab of Simichrome used on the plastic.

Gold nibs are often discolored and may be shined with a polishing cloth used with extremely gentle motions. Ink encrustation on nibs dissolves easily with a dab of saliva, and may be repeated without harming the gold finish. Use extreme care on the bottom portion of the nib as the tiny pellet may be dislodged by accident, thus ruining the nib.

If you find a nicely made pen which needs more repair than mere cleaning and polishing gently, there are many pen "hospitals" that will do the job inexpensively.

Should you find a pen, which you feel may be of a very special type and cannot find information about it, you may write the authors or contact *Pen World,* magazine, listed in the bibliography.

STONE

Treated and fed by a very light rubbing-in of light oil, stone regains its unique color effects and acquires a gloss as it "drinks" the oil into its surface. A light hand should be used here, and only a soft cloth should be used. Tiny chips can be smoothed, as well.

WOOD

Adding lemon oil applications to wooden items is not interference in most cases; it is preservation of the wood. An item that is found outside or in a temperature affected area, such as an attic or basement, might actually require some treatment in order to return it to a condition in which it may be maintained. Spotting of wooden items may often be corrected by applying commercial products, such as Old English Scratch Remover and Polish, with a piece of soft flannel and a light touch.

Should a small section or part of the item be missing or cracked, you may find a local craftsman at a craft fair in your area that might be able to fix it. He might take on the job of carving a new "claw" for an eagle, and may be able to either fill a wide crack or to treat the wood so as to return it to an almost invisible

This desk piece has a letter holder of brass on its top, and a curved surface beneath that contained a partial reproduction of an ancient map. The map was badly discolored by time. It was thoroughly and gently wiped with a damp soft cloth with one drop of a mild dishwashing detergent, until the map was clean.

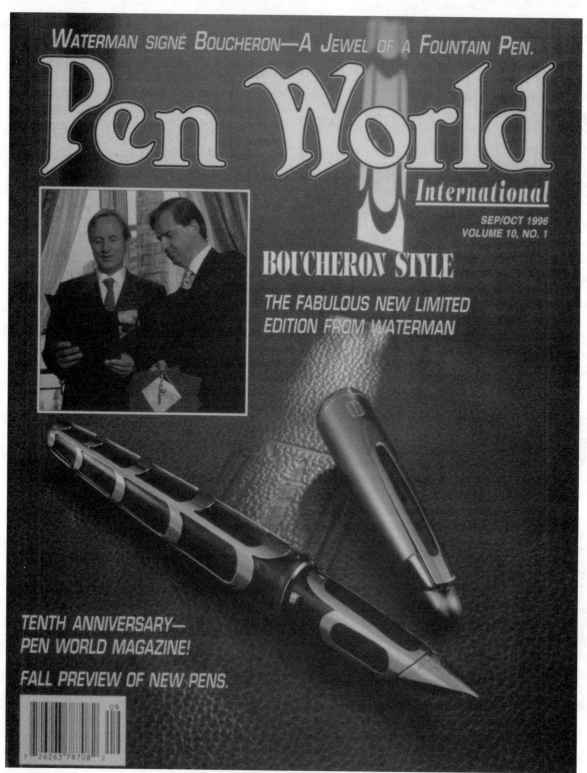

Pen World *provides informative articles and resources for pen and inkwell collectors.*

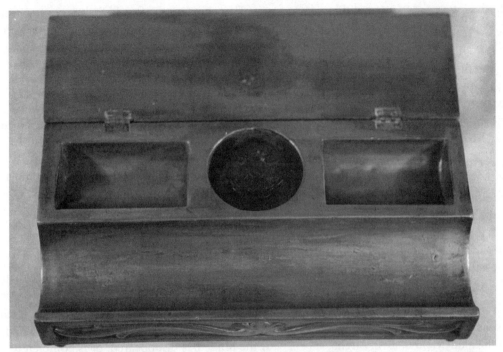

Gold finish on wood, this small home inkstand was completely stained with ink which had been kept in the inkwell space but without a top, as the space is shallow. An older brand of ink with a corked top would have been a better fit. The embedded ink was raised with a soaked, folded washcloth (or a thick piece of towel) that was laid on the wood for ten to fifteen minutes only. Any more would have allowed the wood to swell and perhaps warp the thin, hinged top. Seven soaks were used to lift enough ink to restore the piece to this condition. A soft cloth was used to brighten the gold, which had apparently been rubbed into the wood when the piece was new.

The same inkstand with the lid closed. A thick layer of wax had been deposited on the curved pen-rest about 1/8 inch thick. This had to be gently scraped with a curved metal piece until the wood was free of wax. A gentle polish with clean flannel restored the piece to its present beauty.

width. Usually it is wise not to attempt this yourself, unless you are familiar with the required techniques.

Stripping the finish on wood items should be approached with extreme caution. The cost of the work may be more than the item is worth and, unless the job is extremely professional, the item may be more damaged by such treatment.

If a large portion of the item is stained, consult the yellow pages for an expert in furniture restoration. A professional may either be able to fix the problem or contribute advice so that you can do the work yourself. Ink stains on wood are troublesome and all too common. It is almost impossible to remove this type stain yourself, and should only be handled by an expert.

Nail polish is sometimes found on a wooden item, and if it does not yield to a very light lifting with a fingernail, talk to a person familiar with antique furnishings before trying such shock therapy as nail polish remover. It may do the trick and be what the expert would do, but it can also bleach the piece or cause the wood's finish to curdle and bubble.

NEVER attack unknown clumps of substance on a wooden inkwell or other desk item with an x-acto type knife. The results can be appalling.

Do remember that wood, like all organic materials, needs to be "fed" to be maintained in good condition. Light oils should be used, not commercial spray polishes. Polish is best applied with elbow grease and caution.

METALS

Metals may respond to a light cleaning with light machine oil, but if the item is of precious metal, copper, brass, or bronze, this should be done only with the advice of a jeweler. Removing the "greenish" tones of age from copper or bronze may be an error, as it is just this patina which lends itself to the ambiance of the antique piece.

Fast shine products sold for silver may bring ruinous results, as they may damage other parts of the piece. These products actually remove a thin layer of the metal and immersion in such cleansing products can be a bad mistake.

A fairly stiff paintbrush may be used to remove layers of dirt and dust from the crevices of a metal piece. Once the metal is gently cleaned, the best procedure is to rub it with a special metal polishing cloth available at most antique shops or hobby shops.

Your local hobby shop will be able to provide advice on the best type of glue to reattach any loose piece.

Hinges are often found on antique inkwells. If the piece is found with a broken hinge, or a missing hingepin, a pin or thin finishing nail can often be added if this is the only repair needed. If the hinge has disappeared, or is completely ruined, you may find a local metal company that could inexpensively reconstruct a new hinge for you. We found a local company specializing in

Small brass inkwell stand and matching rocker blotter. The highly shined surface suggests that they have been cleaned with brass cleaner. It is best to leave them in the condition in which you find them, as cleaning destroys the patina of age, and may actually reduce the price of the item. Ink which has dried on the metal surface, may be moistened with a damp Q-tip and gently blotted until it is gone. Inkwell with Lincoln drape design: $60-70, rocker blotter: $35 amd up. Marked Geo. Broch on base.

the repair of church communion equipment and candlesticks which was able to provide the tiny hinges that characterize these items, and make them look as if they had always been part of the piece. Larger cities will have such a company, as does St. Louis.

Inlay defects require expert advice, which may be gained from any art museum or gallery.

Dents in metal items can be a significant problem. If the metal is not very thick, take the piece to a company specializing in repair of brass musical instruments, as they have methods to remove dents from trumpets and saxophones, which may also work with your metal item.

Polishing may be done with several specialized products such as metal cleaners containing polish, but the best polish jobs are done with soft flannel and, again, elbow grease.

Telescoping dip pen/pencil combinations, a special favorite of ours, should not be repaired or restored except by a jeweler.

POTTERY AND CHINA

Many ancient pottery items have cracks, which have darkened with age, and for the most part should be left alone. Some thin cracks may be lightened with a q-tip dipped in bleach, and if the piece is plain, unglazed and very solid, a fast soaking in warm water and bleach may remove some of the darkness of the cracks. Pieces which have decal work or handpainted portions may be severely damaged by such soaking however, so that it is best to leave them as is, or use as little "fixing" as you can. A ceramics shop may be able to provide some good advice in certain cases.

Chips or broken pieces should also be taken to a ceramics expert for advice before attempting to repair or restore them yourself. Some tiny defects in highly glazed porcelain or china pieces have been repaired with a delicate application of clear fingernail polish but it should not be attempted if the defect is larger than a small fleck.

Ceramic glues may be used in some cases, but pressure should be applied lightly to hold the piece in perfect position while drying for 24 hours or more. This light pressure can be provided by the larger post office variety of rubber band. Some ceramic companies may be able to fashion a small replacement piece for items slightly damaged or missing a chip.

Pieces restored in these ways should be described as "restored" when reselling them, and black light will reveal such repairs accurately.

GLASS

Glass inserts for inkwells and inkstands are one of the most vexing problems facing any collector. Usually, a thorough rummage through trays of small parts will turn up one insert now and then.

New inserts may be ordered from a provider, who advertises in the Stained Finger Newsletter, but they are not the originals, nor do they come in all sizes.

It has been a constant surprise to us to find some inserts of incorrect sizes jammed into small inkwells, or small ones rattling around in large inkwells. It is also gratifying when the correct size is found in an antique piece and is of obvious antique vintage. A real surprise has been the number of opal glass inserts, cobalt blue or light green in some European inkstands, and ceramic inserts of all shades of off-white in many very early examples of American inkstands.

Glass inkwells which have a tiny "chigger bite" or fleck missing from an opening or neck may be smoothed with a fine 00 or 000 emery paper. This removes the possibility that the piece may be further damaged or that a finger may be cut by the rough edge of the chip.

A broken glass piece may be repaired if necessary, and an art glass company or even a mirror manufacturer may be able to advise which fixatives or glues should be used. Old

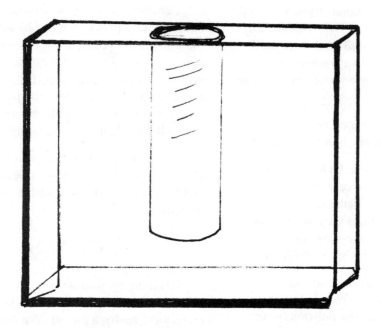

Tiny chips, as indicated in the lower right corner of the sketch, may be smoothed easily with a piece of 000 emery paper. These small chips are known as "chiggerbites."

glue which has turned yellow may be gently soaked free in a lukewarm water bath, then the piece may be completely dried and re-glued with the type of fixative recommended by the glass company. A light but firm pressure should be applied while the newly glued piece is drying, and at least 24 hours should be taken for the drying process. Again, thicker post office rubber bands make fine pressure applicators.

For a replacement of an entire section, it would be best to locate a glassblower or art glass craftsperson for advice and assistance.

The most wanted glass inkwell part is the snail-shaped ink container that graced a popular type of inkwell. Should you locate one of these, be sure to buy it and take it home, for there are four dozen buyers ready and willing to purchase it from you for their own restoration work!

PAPER

Many paper items, such as advertising blotters and antique calendars, may be discolored or torn slightly. An expert in the art prints of R. Atkinson Fox advises that an overnight soaking in a new cat litter pan filled with cool water and a few drops of bleach may help to remove stains and discoloration from calendars, but it is not a method that should be used on blotters. The item should have the water bath poured off and left in the pan to dry before attempting to remove it. Trying to pull a wet piece of paper from such a water bath may guarantee that it will tear and be ruined completely. Mildew may respond to the same treatment.

Storage of paper items is also a problem, and if they are already discolored, placing them in plastic not improved them. If you plan to use plastic to store old magazine ads, calendars, post cards or advertising blotters, go to a comic-book shop and purchase acid-free bags. If they do not carry the largest size, a newspaper such as the Antique Trader Weekly may carry ads for the larger sizes of acid-free plastics.

Calendars should be stored flat in such plastic envelopes, or rolled gently and placed in mailing tubes with identifying labels affixed to the outside. Bubble wrap is recommended for not only storage of these items, but for preparing them for shipping. Most grocery stores are more than willing to supply old apple boxes which are sturdy, stackable, and hold a nice amount of items. Most varieties have hand-grips so that they may be easily lifted. We use many of these when exhibiting our collection.

Displaying Your Collection

Fountain pens may be kept in the flat boxes used by antique dealers to display costume jewelry. They have glass lids that allow the item to be easily viewed. If you intend to show a collection on a wall, special shadow-box frames may be purchased or may be custom made by a frame shop.

In general, the collector will find that there are many experts available for help and advice not only in repair and restoration, but in displaying and maintaining items for a collection. The wise collector or dealer has only to look around for help, advice, and assistance, no matter where he or she lives.

Remember that pricing in most antique guides generally refers to mint items, and is often dependent on auction prices on the West and East Coast. If your piece is not mint (and it hardly ever is) and you live in Dubuque, such prices may be totally unrealistic. If your goal is

to get the best value when either buying or selling antiques, take advantage of special newspapers and collector clubs that may be found in the local library or on the Internet. Use care in buying from Internet sources, and request referrals from past customers of the company. Any reputable dealer or firm will be happy to supply such references.

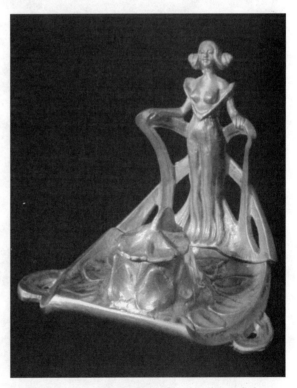

WARNING! This inkstand is lovely and desirable, but it is a reproduction piece. The tab feet have mold-flanges, which narrow them, and the details of the lovely Art Nouveau lady are not as sharp as on the original. It is often missing its inkwell lid or glass insert. Price $45 new as a decoration for your desk. Several hundreds if the real thing.

Glass front wall-display cabinet from a pen store, plus a display-board mounted beneath. Glass will keep your pens from rust, mold, and dust. Keep pens out of sunlight as it will bleach out black rubber and may affect even colorful plastics.

CHAPTER 10

CONCLUSION

Whether your taste runs to inkwells, inkstands and standishes, advertising blotters, ink bottles, pens, or other desk furnishings, there remains a huge amount of collectible material still in storehouses, basements, and attics. Even the lowly calculator, check protector, adding machine, and typewriter have their fanciers.

While my husband and I began our collection with the fountain pen, advanced to the plethora of inkwells and stands, and on into whatever piece of interesting and often unique writing materials came our way; one thing we have learned is that one person's junk is another person's treasure! One only has to visit a paper collectible show to see visitors of all ages poring over files of detached pages containing advertisements for perfume, vintage automobiles, ink, fountain pens and other items to understand the amazing variety of interests in the collectible field. These crumbling old pages are themselves priced from fifty cents to as much as twelve dollars, depending on what product is displayed, and whether color or artwork is included.

As long as items belonging to our ancestors exist, we, the inheritors of such a rich and varied history of invention, will continue to seek them out, repair, restore, display, or just enjoy these vestiges of the past.

Our advice to you is to ENJOY your collection, whatever it may be. We do not urge you to buy "only the best," as these "best" examples may be very high in price, and your budget may be slim. Acquiring a piece that may not be perfect or as desirable as a Bradley and Hubbard bronze or a Tiffany art glass sample might be a bit less exciting when you are beginning, but there are several things to remember. First, your items may be unique and will be a point of pride in your collection in years to come. Secondly, an item of lesser value may be traded to another collector for an item you prefer, especially if you have been lucky enough to find two examples of a certain piece and are willing to let one go. Third, you may find that once you have bought an inexpensive but complete item, it may grow in charm and be the centerpiece of a fine collection.

When we began collecting pens, we purchased many "no-name" pens and many Sheaffer pens of little value. As our collection grew and our acumen increased, we were able to trade groups of these pens for one perfect pen we really desired. I have traded a fairly large collection of one particular type of pen to the emerging sculptor and artist D.J. Kennedy for one of his extremely desirable hand-fashioned fountain pens.

We highly recommend that you attend local antique fairs, and if possible, the yearly inkwells convention specializing in writing artifacts as well as inkwells and inkstands. Pen shows are held in many large cities several times year, and there are always dealers accessory items such as inkwells at every show. Perhaps we'll see you at one of these.

Good Hunting!

Beverly and Raymond Jaegers

St. Louis, Missouri   1999

BIBLIOGRAPHY AND RESOURCES

Books and Articles

Badders, Veldon *Collectors Guide to Inkwells, Identification and Values.* Paducah, Kentucky: Collector Books, 1995.

---. *Collectors Guide to Inkwells, Identification and Values, Volume II.* Paducah, Kentucky: Collector Books, 1997.

Bowen, Glen. *Collectible Fountain Pens.* Gas City, Indiana: LW Book Sales, 1982.

Covill, William E., Jr. *Ink Bottles and Inkwells.* Taunton, Massachusetts: William S. Sullwold, 1971.

Fischler, George and Schneider, Stuart. *Fountain Pens and Pencils.* West Chester, Pennsylvania: Schiffer Publishing, 1990.

"Fountain Pens, Trash or Treasure," *Antique Trader Weekly.* 1995.

Jaegers, Beverly and Raymond. "The Exciting History of Inkwells," *Pen World*, March, 1996.

Koch, Robert. *Louis C. Tiffany's Glass–Bronzes–Lamps.* New York: Crown Publishers, Inc., 1971.

Lawrence, Cliff. *An Illustrated Pen History.* Dunedin, Florida: Pen Fanciers Club, 1986.

Rivera, Betty and Ted *Inkstands and Inkwells.* New York: Crown Publishers 1973.

Unknown. *Pens, Inks and Inkstands.* London: 1858.

Periodicals and Organizations

The Antique Trader Weekly, POB 1050, Dubuque, IA 52004-1050, subscriptions $35.00 per year

American Pencil Collectors Society, M&V Hodson, POB 441, Roosevelt, AZ 85545, APCS Newsletter and membership $10.00 per year

Paper & Advertising Collector, POB 500, Mount Joy, PA 17552, subscription $15.00 per year

Penfinder, Berliner Pen, 928 Broadway, Suite 604, New York, NY 10010, subscriptions $12.00 per year.

Pen World Magazine, World Publications, POB 6007, Kingswood, TX 77339, subscriptions $42.00 per year.

The Stained Finger/The Society of Inkwell Collectors, 5136 Thomas Avenue South,

Minneapolis, MN 55410, subscriptions $22.50 per year

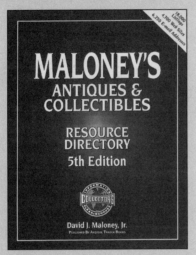

 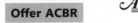

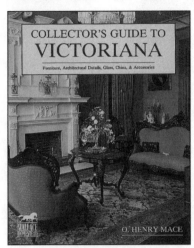

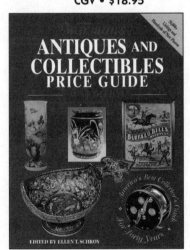
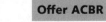